LEADING WITH INSIGHT

31 DAYS OF WISDOM FOR LEADERS

CORY LEE

Inscript

BLADENSBURG, MARYLAND

Jeremiah 33:3

Requests for permission can be addressed to Inscript Books, a division of Dove Christian Publishers, P.O. Box 611, Bladensburg, MD 20710-0611, www.inscriptpublishing.com.

Paperback ISBN: 978-1-957497-27-3

Inscript and the portrayal of a pen with script are trademarks of Dove Christian Publishers.

Published in the United States of America

This book is dedicated to my wife, Kimberly Lee, whose unwavering love and support knows no bounds. Your belief in my dreams and relentless encouragement have ignited my passion, propelled me to new heights, and have drawn me closer to The Heart of The Father.

Contents

Introduction

Leadership is the ability to influence others. You may lead a large corporation or a small department or division. You may lead a small business, a family unit, or a community group, or you may lead a Sunday School class. No matter the role you find yourself in, the fact remains that you have an influence on someone. This devotional, based on the wisdom found in the book of Proverbs, was written to help you become the type of leader others will follow because of who you are, what you represent, and Who you are led by.

The book of Proverbs is primarily written by King Solomon of Israel, with a few other contributors. The word "Proverb" in Hebrew is 'mashal' and has two meanings. The first is what we typically think of as a proverb; it's a parable, a metaphor, or a pithy saying that expresses wisdom. The second definition in Hebrew is a homonym. It can mean to rule, to take dominion, or to reign in power. Proverbs 8 of TPT[1] says this: "I empower kings to reign and rulers to make laws that are just. I empower princes to rise and take dominion, and generous ones to govern the earth."

In 1 Chronicles 22:8-10, the word of The Lord came to King David as he was lamenting the loss of his son with Bathsheba. The Lord told David that he would have another son named Solomon that would become the next king of Israel. Before Solomon was conceived, he had a call of leadership on his life. Once Solomon was born, David and Bathsheba began to teach him how to act and think like a king. From an early age, he was taught how to

---

1   Scripture marked TPT is taken from The Passion Translation®. Copyright © 2017, 2018, 2020 by Passion & Fire Ministries, Inc. Used by permission. All rights reserved. ThePassionTranslation.com.

make leadership decisions and properly rule, reign, and lead the Lord's people. From birth, Solomon did not receive the typical Hebrew school teaching of the day. From a young age, he was taught to think and make decisions like a leader. On the surface, these Proverbs may appear to be wise sayings or motivational quotes. Still, they are much more than motivational phrases. They are Spirit-filled, and the Spirit of our Lord has breathed upon every line and every word of this incredible book. As you read the book of Proverbs, filter your reading through a leadership lens to gain principles of leading others well and making wise decisions.

In 1 Kings 3, God comes at night to King Solomon and asks him, "What shall I give you?" Solomon asks for an understanding mind and discernment between good and evil to govern the Lord's people well. Solomon could have asked for wealth, he could have asked for power, he could have asked for anything in the world, yet when asked by the Creator what he desired most, King Solomon asked for wisdom so he could lead well.

As you lead, you can rely on the wisdom found in this world, you can rely on your own intellect, or you can rely on the wisdom from above that comes from the Holy Spirit, the Spirit of the Living God, who resides in every believer. Check out what Paul says in 1 Corinthians 2:6-16:

> *6 Yet when I am among mature believers, I do speak with words of wisdom, but not the kind of wisdom that belongs to this world or to the rulers of this world, who are soon forgotten. 7 No, the wisdom we speak of is the mystery of God[c]—his plan that was previously hidden, even though he made it for our ultimate glory before the world began. 8 But the rulers of this world have not understood it; if they had, they would not have crucified our glorious Lord. 9 That is what the Scriptures mean when they say,*

> *"No eye has seen, no ear has heard,*
> * and no mind has imagined*
> *what God has prepared*
> * for those who love him."[d]*

Introduction

[10] But[c] it was to us that God revealed these things by his Spirit. For his Spirit searches out everything and shows us God's deep secrets. [11] No one can know a person's thoughts except that person's own spirit, and no one can know God's thoughts except God's own Spirit. [12] And we have received God's Spirit (not the world's spirit), so we can know the wonderful things God has freely given us.

[13] When we tell you these things, we do not use words that come from human wisdom. Instead, we speak words given to us by the Spirit, using the Spirit's words to explain spiritual truths. [14] But people who aren't spiritual can't receive these truths from God's Spirit. It all sounds foolish to them, and they can't understand it, for only those who are spiritual can understand what the Spirit means. [15] Those who are spiritual can evaluate all things, but they themselves cannot be evaluated by others. [16] For,

"Who can know the Lord's thoughts?
 Who knows enough to teach him?"

But we understand these things, for we have the mind of Christ.

You have the mind of Christ, and, as you read these daily devotionals, draw near to Him, and He will draw near to you; call to Him, and He will answer you and tell you great and unsearchable things, things that you do not know. This devotional will help you as a leader draw near to the Holy Spirit and lead with wisdom not found in this world so you can impact the lives of those you lead and advance the Kingdom of our Lord.

Day 1

Understand Followership

Fear of The Lord is the foundation of true knowledge, but fools despise wisdom and discipline. Proverbs 1:7 NLT²

How then does a man gain the essence of wisdom? We cross the threshold of true knowledge when we live in obedient devotion to God. Stubborn know-it-alls will never stop to do this, for they scorn true wisdom and knowledge. Proverbs 1:7 TPT

Proverbs 1 says that understanding these proverbs will empower you to reign in life and teach leaders wisdom and discipline, helping them understand the insights of the wise and how to live disciplined and successful lives, doing what is right, just, and fair. According to The Passion Translation, here are some benefits leaders will receive when these proverbs become more than just head knowledge but embedded into their hearts:

- Revelation of wisdom.
- Impartation of Spiritual understanding.
- Keys to unlocking the treasures of true knowledge.
- Ability to demonstrate wisdom in every relationship.
- Choosing what is just, right, and fair.

---

2 Scripture quotations marked NLT are taken from the Holy Bible, New Living Translation, copyright © 1996, 2004, 2015 by Tyndale House Foundation. Used by permission of Tyndale House Publishers, Inc., Carol Stream, Illinois 60188. All rights reserved.

- Gives great skill to teach the immature and to make them wise.
- Gives youth an understanding of their design and destiny.
- Acquire brilliant strategies for leadership.

That is an impressive list of benefits. So, how can a leader gain this kind of wisdom and these benefits? The answer is found in verse 7 of chapter 1; the beginning of wisdom is the fear of the Lord. The fear of the Lord is a reverential awe and living in devotion to Him. The contrast to the fear of the Lord is the fear of man. Isaiah 51:12-13 says, "I, yes I, am the one who comforts you. So why are you afraid of mere humans who wither like the grass and disappear? Yet you have forgotten the Lord, your Creator, the one who stretched out the sky like a canopy and laid the foundations of the earth. Will you remain in constant dread of human oppressors? Will you continue to fear the anger of your enemies? Where is their fury and anger now?"

The very beginning of Kingdom wisdom is to live your life in the awe and reverential fear of the Lord. Oswald Chambers said, "When you fear God, you fear nothing else, whereas if you do not fear God, you fear everything else."

The fear of man is a fear trap that many leaders fall into. Now we as leaders would never verbalize it like that, but we do concern ourselves with the thoughts and opinions of others instead of what the Lord is saying. We fear man's approval or disapproval instead of seeking God's approval. What we fear is a clue as to what we trust. If we fear the opinions of others, then that is a clue as to where our trust lies. Our Father is good and has good plans and thoughts toward you, but He is also the creator of all things. So, why should we fear mere human beings?

The very foundation of increasing in wisdom is built upon the reverential fear of God. An interesting balance is having love for the Father and having a reverential fear of Him. He desires intimacy and deep connection, but this desire is not for us to do as we please. I heard author and leader John Bevere tell a story of when he got the opportunity to meet a world-famous minister who ended up behind bars after being convicted of some terrible crimes. While meeting with this minister, John asked him a pointed question: "When did you stop loving Jesus?" The minister's response was a real eye-opener. He declared that his love for Jesus never wavered, not even for a moment, despite being fully aware of the sins he was committing. He said, "I never stopped loving Jesus, but I did stop fearing the Lord."

If this is the starting point of wisdom and all these incredible blessings, then our first step is to assess our personal view of God. The next step is to simply ask! James 1:5-8 says ask without doubting, and the Lord will give His wisdom generously and ungrudgingly. One of my favorite verses is Jeremiah 33:3; it says, "Call to me and I will answer you and tell you great and incomprehensible things you do not know."

There is so much more to this life and the world than what we see with our physical eyes. We have a good Father who wants to give us good things, but if we have a heart of arrogance and pride, we most likely will never humble ourselves to ask of Him in complete faith.

As you continue to read the book of Proverbs, you will see that wisdom is personified as a woman, and her call is constant in everyday life. Yet we often tune out her call or simply cannot hear it because we are so busy. The time to tune our hearts and ears is now; her call is now, so the time to listen is now. Understanding how to listen will enable you to learn to follow and lead others well. Only when we understand how to follow will we know the experience of being under authority.

Civilization is always in danger when those who have never learned to obey are given the right to command. -Fulton J. Sheen.

What is the first thing that comes to mind when you think about God? Ask the Holy Spirit to reveal how you see the Father and ask Him what the Truth is. Then ask the Father how He sees you.

Do you practice slowing down to listen and for regular rest?

What do you feel like the Lord is saying to you in this season?

Day 2

"I WILL!"

"My son, if you accept my words and store up my commands within you, 2 turning your ear to wisdom and applying your heart to understanding—3 indeed, if you call out for insight and cry aloud for understanding, 4 and if you look for it as for silver and search for it as for hidden treasure, 5 then you will understand the fear of the Lord and find the knowledge of God. 6 For the Lord gives wisdom; from his mouth come knowledge and understanding. 7 He holds success in store for the upright, he is a shield to those whose walk is blameless, 8 for he guards the course of the just and protects the way of his faithful ones. 9 Then you will understand what is right and just and fair—every good path. 10 For wisdom will enter your heart, and knowledge will be pleasant to your soul. 11 Discretion will protect you, and understanding will guard you. -Proverbs 2:1-11

Proverbs 2 starts off with a question: will you receive My words? That's His infallible written word of scripture, those Holy Spirit-inspired unctions, prophetic words spoken to you, and any other way He communicates to you. Will you receive it? But the question also asks, will you honor and treasure His word? Not treating His word as something common but as you would treat something of exceedingly great value. So, when God speaks, how well do you receive and honor what He says?

I've found that the more I honor and treat what He says as

holy, the more I hear from Him, and the more clearly I hear from Him. Verse 2 in TPT says, "Train your heart to listen when I speak." It's getting to know the sound of His voice.

We have three children, and I know each of their voices well. If you and I were out together having a cup of coffee and one of them gave me a call, I could immediately discern which of the three I was talking with. If you had not met any of our children or spent much time with them, you would have difficulty discerning which of the three you were speaking with.

It's training our ears, eyes, and heart to understand when He speaks because He speaks in many ways. I recently read in Exodus 3, where God speaks to Moses through the burning bush. Scripture says that Moses was in the wilderness with a flock of sheep, and he noticed a bush was on fire, but it did not burn up, so he was like, "Hmm, that's interesting. Let me go over there and check that out." Scripture then says, "When the Lord saw that he had gone over to look, God called to him from the bush." Something interesting caught Moses' eye, and he gave his attention to it. It was only when he gave his attention to the bush that God began to speak.

We train our hearts to listen by engaging in conversations when those unctions catch our attention. When I read a scripture or a word in a certain verse and something about that word or verse jumps out to me, that's an invitation to a conversation. That's where I begin to seek it out like treasure; I tune my heart and ask Holy Spirit what He is saying.

In verse 3, it says to call out for insight and wisdom. The book of James says that if ANYONE lacks wisdom, then simply ask. So, what's the culmination of seeking wisdom, treasuring His word, treasure hunting for insight, discernment, and understanding? Well...it's the fear of the Lord and finding knowledge of God.

That's the culmination....an understanding that the fear of The Lord is to be a reverential awe and worship of the very One who spoke and creation burst forth, the One who marked off the dimensions of the earth and set its footings, the One who told the seas just how far they could go and not a millimeter further, the One who said to the waves HALT! The One who tells the sun when to rise and when to set. That very One created you on purpose and, above all else, desires a personal and intimate relationship with you. That fact is true for you; it is also true for every individual you lead and influence.

Job 38:32 says he has a storehouse of snow and hail and knows how to disperse lightning. That's simply amazing! The opposite of the fear of God is the fear of man. When we do not fear God, we fear man. When we focus on what others may approve or disapprove of rather than what God does, we respond to their voices rather than His. Bill Johnson says, "If I don't live for the praise of men, then I won't die by their criticism."

Inclining our hearts to hear His voice helps us to gain knowledge of God. This knowledge is intimate, not just knowing of or about God, but knowing His heart and ways. It's understanding what He has done, His heart behind it, and what He desires to do today. I can read His word, memorize every single verse in the Bible, and have a head full of knowledge and facts, but it's when I encounter, interact, and engage with the Author that I gain a heart of understanding and I become transformed.

Why is all of that important for a leader? Because transformation begins with me. As I become transformed as a leader, then I can bring transformation to others. Leading others is both caught and taught. The taught part is the information or knowledge that we teach and train. Anyone can do that. But the truly great leaders deposit something into those they lead and train. They do not simply give head knowledge alone or attempt to stimulate their mind only, but they pierce the heart by the Spirit in which they do it; that is the caught part. As a leader, you are contagious. The people under your influence are catching something from you. When they are in your presence, what are you depositing into them that they carry on when they leave your presence?

Are people catching hope, enthusiasm, initiative, self-worth, passion, or the love of the Father? Or do people walk away with indifference, anger, pride, or selfishness?

Allow the Holy Spirit to be so strong within you that the light of our Lord Jesus Christ burns so brightly that it causes others to leave your presence and say, "Wow, there is something different about that man or woman right there."

Day 3

"Unfair Advantage"

"Never let loyalty and kindness leave you! Tie them around your neck as a reminder. Write them deep within your heart. There you will find favor with both God and people, and you will earn a good reputation."
Proverbs 3:3-4

These are amazing words of wisdom. When we allow love and faithfulness to become a part of who we are, they are written on the tablet of our hearts and become our operating system or default mode. This leads to favor and a good reputation with both God and man. Samuel became one of the most recognized prophets in the Old Testament. 1 Samuel 2:26 says that he continued to grow in stature and favor with the Lord and people. Luke 2:52 says that Jesus Himself grew in wisdom and stature and favor with God and man.

The Hebrew word translated as "good reputation" is actually defined as shrewdness, insight, or understanding. This really implies that when we make love and faithfulness our default mode, our reputation is winning at life. Think about that for a moment; when we are led by love and faithfulness, we receive favor. Favor is defined as showing approval or preference toward, giving unfair preferential treatment, or an act of kindness beyond what is due.

I do not know about you, but preferential treatment toward me or acts of kindness beyond expectations from our Father and the people of this world would really help me in my leadership. I think it's obvious that we would want to grow in our relationship with the Father and see the resulting favor, but we may not consider the need to have favor with people. However, it's just as important.

We cannot lead people that we do not have influence with. For us to truly lead people to their potential and for our teams to do great things, people must like and want to help us. When those we lead have doubts about trusting us, there will also be doubts about their willingness to give their best. As leaders, we must be able to answer three questions that all followers have:

1. Do you care for me? That's a question of the heart. Do you actually like me is the question. People can tell if we are just putting up with and tolerating them or truly caring about them. It will come across in how we engage, interact, and offer opportunities.

2. Can you help me? People want to be on winning teams, and this question really means, "If I come underneath your leadership, will I improve? Will I see growth? Can you help me be bigger and better than I currently am?"

3. Can I trust you? This third question means, "Can I trust you enough to give you my very best?" Trust is a two-way street, but as the leader, it begins with you. If you prove to be a leader unworthy of trust, those you lead will always hold back and never give their best.

What if we started our relationships by trusting those we lead instead of them having to first prove their trust? It would probably change how we engage and interact, but I also believe it would change the expectations. Most leaders I know start with no trust and act as if they must prove trust. Let's flip that model. I like how John Maxwell says it: "I put a 10 on everyone's head. I put a 10 on your head, but you are the one that takes it off." So, start with trust and let others prove or disprove that trust instead of starting out with no trust and making those you lead earn it. I know what you may be thinking. If I do that, what if they take advantage of me or try to accuse me, use me, or abuse me? Well, the reality is that when we open ourselves up, some will take advantage of us. But the majority will not.

"People are often unreasonable, irrational, and self-centered. Forgive them anyway. If you are kind, people may accuse you of selfish, ulterior motives, be kind anyway. If you are successful, you will win some unfaithful friends and some genuine enemies. Succeed anyway. If you are honest and sincere, people may deceive you. Be honest and sincere anyway. What you spend years creating, others could destroy overnight. Create anyway. If you find serenity and happiness, some may be jealous. Be happy anyway. The good you do today will often be forgotten. Do good anyway. Give the best you have, and it will never be enough. Give your best anyway. In the final analysis, it is between you and God. It was never between you and them anyway."-Mother Teresa

We are Christ's ambassadors, especially to those we lead. We are to represent Him and His Kingdom. An ambassador is an accredited diplomat a country sends to another country as its official representative. When that ambassador goes to another country, they represent the country that sent them. However, if a foreign government does not approve of or like the ambassador, they can declare the person a *persona non grata* or an unacceptable person. Bind loyalty and kindness around your neck. Be bigger on the inside than on the outside.

We want to become men and women of influence who others willfully follow because of who we are and Who we represent.

Do you naturally trust people? Why or why not?

Do you trust yourself?

Would you follow you?

Day 4

The Price Tag of Wisdom

"Wisdom is the most valuable commodity – so buy it! Revelation knowledge is what you need – so invest in it!" - Proverbs 4:7 TPT

Solomon says that wisdom is the most precious commodity, and we should buy it, no matter the price. When we purchase something, money is exchanged for a product or a service. We gladly purchase the things we need and the things we want if we see the value of it. The wisest man said that wisdom is something we should be willing to go all in on. Wisdom does come at a cost; there is a price to pay. Many times, there is a financial price to be paid to gain wisdom. You can pay to attend courses, seminars, and webinars and buy books. You can even pay other leaders to coach and mentor you. A few people are willing to pay that price, and I am one of them. I am all in and gladly pay that price because I know the value of gaining wisdom. But there is a higher plane to this price that many leaders are unwilling to pay, and that is spending alone time with the Father in the secret place. The price is us willing to slow down, be still, and sit in the presence of the Lord.

In our busyness and the doingness of our lives, the price of slowing down is viewed as too expensive, but this is the price associated with true wisdom. Wisdom can come from books, courses, seminars, webinars, etc. There is wisdom that can be found in this world and from man, but there is also wisdom that you will not find in this world.

"Yet when I am among mature believers, I do speak with

words of wisdom, but not the kind of wisdom that belongs to this world or to the rulers of this world, who are soon forgotten." 1 Corinthians 2:6

Proverbs 3:32 TPT says. "He brings the upright into His confidence," implying that He gives His private counsel. Proverbs 2:7 says that the Lord has a hidden storehouse of wisdom that is made available to all His Godly ones. If we just come to the door longing for a word, it will be given to us. Jesus says ask, and you will receive, seek and you will find, knock and the door will be opened.

Our Father is into relationships, not religion. God wants to throw all His wisdom upon you, but more than anything, He wants our hearts, so much that He sent His son Jesus to die for our sins so we could be one with Him.

Psalm 103 says that Moses knew the ways of God, and the children of Israel knew His acts. The children of Israel saw what God did and witnessed His acts, but Moses knew why. That's because Moses intentionally spent time with God and spoke with Him face-to-face as a friend.

So, what do we practically do?

Be intentional about spending time with God. Make that time a priority in your life, not something we do when we can if we can. Get into His Word and listen for His voice. He speaks in many different ways. Just one of those ways is through Scripture. You may notice a word or phrase that just jumps out at you for some reason. That is an invitation to a conversation.

Proverbs 4:23 gives us another way. Above all else, guard your heart, for everything you do flows from it. Your heart is the seat of all your emotions, will, opinions, perceptions, and beliefs. Your beliefs drive your behavior. You guard your heart by being intentional with what we allow into our eye gates, our ear gates, and with whom we associate. It is so important for us to watch what we allow in.

If you have children, you'll want to monitor whom they spend time with and what they watch and listen to. Why is that? It's because you know that those things will influence their behavior. At what point is that no longer true? The answer is that it is *always* true. What we watch and listen to as adults will influence our beliefs, opinions, perspectives, and values. So, what is shaping your heart? Is it culture or Scripture? Is it the world or the Word?

Paul said to take each thought captive, but in my book, "Heart of The Father," I share how studies show that, on average, a person has between 30,000-60,000 thoughts per day. Of those thoughts, 95% of them are the same exact thoughts they had the day before, which are the same exact thoughts they had the day before that.

My encouragement for today is to become aware of what we are thinking about and be intentional about what we allow in through our eyes and ears. There is also wisdom, understanding, and insight that is available, but something even greater is available, and that's a deep, abiding, and intimate relationship with the Father.

DAY 5

The Most Boring Key to Success

"For the ways of man are before the eyes of the Lord, And He ponders all his paths. ²² His own iniquities entrap the wicked man, And he is caught in the cords of his sin." – Proverbs 5:21-22 NKJV³

For God sees everything you do and his eyes are wide open as he observes every single habit you have. Beware that your sins don't overtake you and that the scars of your own conscience don't become the ropes that tie you up. – Proverbs 5:21-22 TPT

In verse 21, we see that everything is laid bare before the Lord, that He sees all, and that nothing is hidden from Him. Second Chronicles 16:9 says that the eyes of the Lord move to and fro throughout the earth so that He may support those whose heart is completely His. Our Father is searching the land, and He's looking at hearts. Proverbs 5:21 uses the word *paths* in NKJV, and in TPT, the same word is *habits*. So, this proverb is about those acts that we habitually do; it's literally those ruts in a road caused by repeated travel of wagons. Our leadership wisdom for today is all about our habits. Are the actions that we do regularly becoming cords that bind and carry us away as kidnapped captives robbed of destiny, or do we have habits leading us toward the purpose for which God created us?

---

3   Scripture marked NKJV taken from the New King James Version®. Copyright © 1982 by Thomas Nelson. Used by permission. All rights reserved.

If I were sitting down with you, and, throughout our conversation, I asked you, "What are some requirements for someone to be successful?" What would you say? Would you say hard work ethic? A good attitude? Some good luck? Have high intelligence? Good communication skills?

If I could pinpoint just one thing that has led to any success that I have had, it's the topic of this chapter. In fact, you will find every successful person in any field has this same thing in common, but before you read on for this one thing, I have one more question for you. If I gave you a choice between taking a briefcase of $3,000,000 right now or a penny that doubles itself every day for 31 days, which would you choose? Would you take the immediate $3,000,000 or patiently wait to see what the penny does?

If you chose the penny that doubles itself for 31 days, on day 5, you would be sitting at a measly $0.16. On day eleven, you would have finally cracked double digits as you would have $10.24. On day twenty, over half of the month would be complete, and you would have only $5,242.88 compared to the $3,000,000 you could have chosen. However, if you had the patience to wait out the consistency of the penny on day thirty-one, you would have a whopping $10,737,418.23. Wow! That's the power of compounding consistency over time. Never underestimate the power of compounding consistency.

The most boring key to any success is consistency. Consistency is not sexy at all, but here's the deal: motivation will get you going, but discipline keeps you going. Being persistent will help you get it; being consistent will help you keep it. All paths, every single one of them, requires consistency.

Most people are not successful in their business or their role or in their organization, not because they lack opportunity or support or talent, but because they don't understand that to be successful, it requires consistency. See, anybody can be good once, but too many rest on that and make a lifestyle out of what they did in the past.

I like what Jim Rohn says about habits, and he came up with a formula for success and a formula for failure around habits.

"The formula for success is a few simple disciplines practiced every day. The formula for failure is a few errors in judgment repeated every day." The key word in both of those formulas is the word *few*. Neither success nor failure is typically one giant leap or one giant fall but a gradual process. The path to success is always uphill. John Maxwell says that many people have uphill dreams, but they have downhill habits. All of that is true and shows the importance of consistency with our habits. However, we can be consistent in doing the wrong things as well. All the above statements have been written in many other leadership and personal growth books. If you've been leading for a while, you have probably heard most of this already, but what is not written or talked about as often in the lane of leadership and personal growth is that, as leaders, we can also do the right actions with the wrong attitude or heart posture. It's the spirit in which we do the things we do. I would suggest that the spirit in which we do the things we do is much more important than what we do because it reveals our heart. We do not just want to blindly do activities simply to check something off a list. We are Kingdom leaders designed and destined to impact culture.

In Mark 7, the entire culture did these ceremonial washings as an external sign of their purity before they ate, claiming they were now undefiled. It was an act merely performed on the physical plane, but Jesus was about to teach them a much higher Spiritual truth. He sets it up by first calling them hypocrites and then references Isaiah 29:13:

> "These people honor me with their lips, but their hearts are far from me. They worship me in vain; their teachings are merely human rules."

A hypocrite is a play actor or pretender who says or does something but believes the opposite. On the physical plane, they demonstrated a religious custom, but their heart was left unchanged. In Revelation, Jesus tells John to "come up here." He was telling John to view things from a higher plane. We have the mind of Christ and are called to do the same thing. We are to look at our actions and habits to see which we do out of 'religious duty' as opposed to doing out of a pure heart.

In Mark 7:15, Jesus tells the people that nothing outside a person can defile them by going into them. Rather, it is what comes out of a person that defiles them.

In Mark 2, Jesus and His disciples are walking one day when the disciples begin to pick grain on a Sabbath. According to the Jewish interpretation of the law, this was an unlawful action. So, the religious leaders ask why they are doing what is unlawful. Jesus then teaches a higher spiritual truth: the Sabbath was created for man, not vice versa. They had made the Sabbath this burdensome activity when in reality, God instituted the Sabbath as a time to be refreshed, restored, and to spend time in His presence. God created it to encourage our growth in our faith, not a mindless ritual to simply obey rules.

The religious leaders were focused on the form and not the power. They worried more about the rules and how things should be done rather than the greater spiritual truth of drawing nearer to the Father.

Habits are important, but we can also get into the habit of doing the wrong things or even the right things with the wrong heart posture. Habits become bad when we go through the motions of our traditions and spiritual practices, yet they bring no fruit and leave us unchanged. It's a matter of the heart.

During a recent season in my life, I found myself frustrated each time I left church and really could not figure out why I was feeling this way. I went to the Lord in prayer and asked Him why I was feeling the way I did. He immediately asked me a question back. He said, "Why do you [plural, as a group] go to church?" I said, "Well, we go to church to be with other brothers and sisters, we go to worship, we go to be equipped," and I gave a long list that any good churchgoer would give. After I gave my list, He asked me a second question, "Why do you [personally] go to church?" I was a bit taken aback and tried to be honest and sincere and said, "Well, it's something that I have always done; it's just what we do on a Sunday morning; it's what I'm supposed to do." That last statement helped me realize I was going to church out of an assumed obligation. I'm all for going to church and being a part of a local body; please, do not hear me say otherwise. But what I am asking you is, what is the purpose for which you go? What are your intentions for going? I was going because I thought others would shame me for not being there. There is no shame in the Kingdom of God. The Holy Spirit will convict but never condemn, and He was convicting me of improper heart posture. I had taken a spiritual practice and turned it into an obligation.

For you, what spiritual practices or activities have become more of a tradition rather than a matter of the heart?

Where do you think we, as The Body of Christ, have done this?

Day 6

The Wisdom from the Tiny Ant

"When you are feeling lazy come learn this lesson from this tale of the tiny ant. Yes, all you lazy bones come learn from the example of the ant and enter into wisdom. The ants have no chief, no boss, no manager – no one has to tell them what to do. You'll see them working and toiling all summer long, stockpiling their food in preparation for winter. So wake up sleepyhead! How long will you lie there? When will you wake up and get out of bed? If you keep nodding off and thinking I'll do it later or say to yourself I'll just sit back awhile and take it easy. Just watch how your future unfolds! By making excuses you'll learn what it means to go without. Poverty will pounce on you like a bandit and move in as your roommate for life." – Proverbs 6:6-11 (TPT)

Laziness is the unwillingness to work or use energy or to make excuses to avoid doing what needs to be done. It's procrastinating what needs to be done today. It also refers to being sluggish or the way you go about doing your work with a lack of enthusiasm or the lack of a sense of urgency. The wisdom from the ant is that they intuitively understand the law of sowing and reaping, that each action will produce some kind of result, while no action will produce no result. They are not standing around waiting for someone to tell them what needs to be done. Those who stand around waiting for orders lack self-discipline, but ultimately, they lack vision. They see only at the moment without consideration for the bigger picture. The wisdom from the ant is that they aren't standing around waiting for someone to give them permission to act on what clearly needs to be done. The ant is self-motivated and requires no one to lead or motivate them to act. It's simply within their nature to diligently work and do what's necessary. They do not wait for the stomach to growl; they get to work now because they know it will growl.

A wise leader is a person of action. The wise leader is disciplined. The wise leader makes the most of their time, and they know that their success or lack thereof will be determined by their daily agenda.

One of my early mentors in the personal growth space was motivational teacher Jim Rohn. Jim often spoke about the formula for failure and the formula for success. He said the formula for success was just a few small disciplines practiced daily, while the formula for failure is just a few tiny errors in judgment repeated every day. Check out the word *few* in both formulas. The formula for success is a *few* small disciplines, and the formula for failure is a *few* tiny errors in judgment. Rarely is success one giant leap that results in overnight success, while a huge failure is rarely one giant step off a cliff.

I had a conversation with a friend of mine recently about this topic. He once made a very poor decision which led to a moral failure, but during our conversation, he made an interesting statement. He said the poor decision was where he fell, but two years prior, he stopped keeping his guard up, which is where he began to fall. It was a slow fade that led up to the moment of that failure.

So, I want you to think about the type of leader you want to be. What do you want to be known for? Really think about this, and please do not skip right past taking the time to think about this question.

With that bigger picture in mind, what are some small habits you can implement daily that would help you become that type of leader? These habits should be so simple that they can be performed day in and day out. For me personally, I have narrowed mine down to 5 things that I do every day, whether it's a random

Tuesday or I'm on vacation with my family. These 5 are based on my vision and values and may not apply to you, but I just want to share these with you to serve as an example. Here are my five: each day, I read 10 pages of a book; each day, I create content; each day, I work out; each day, I make time to reflect; and each day, I begin my day in prayer. They are simple to do, but simple things are also simple not to do.

These small actions do not seem to produce much fruit upfront but compound over time. I have learned that those who are successful in any endeavor do consistently what those who are unsuccessful do only occasionally. Unsuccessful or lazy people base their actions on how they feel at a given moment. They make their decisions based on emotion rather than vision. They wait for motivation to strike. The lazy bones has an "I'll wait until" mindset. I'll wait until I feel like it. I'll wait until I get into a position of authority before I start learning leadership. I'll wait until I get enough money before being generous or tithing. I'll wait until I get to a certain point in my career when it stabilizes before I spend more time with my family and friends. But *I'll wait until* is not a strategy for success. The result of *I'll wait until* is poverty pouncing on you like a bandit.

Action precedes motivation. Many people are stuck because they are waiting for motivation to strike, for a sudden lightning bolt of inspiration to fill them to get them moving in the direction of their dreams. They wait for the motivation to come so they can act, but in my experience, the action comes first, then the motivation. Motivation is based on emotion and feeling. There will be days on your journey to success when motivation is low, and you do not feel like doing what's required.

If you see anyone successful in any field, you can be sure they made decisions against their emotions; they acted when they did not feel like taking action. If you see a person with six-pack abs, they decided against themselves to get to the gym when they did not feel like going and to eat certain foods when they really wanted the junk food. If you see a successful businessperson, they have made decisions to invest in themselves and to learn certain skills that sharpen their strengths when they could have chosen to settle. Successful leaders do not wait for motivation to come, and they do not allow motivation or the lack of it to determine whether they'll do what's required. Besides, what if the motivation never comes?

What type of leader do you want to be? What do you want to be known for?

What do you need to start doing?

What do you need to stop doing?

Day 7

The Apple of My Eye

"Keep my commands and live and my law as the apple of your eye." -Proverbs 7:2

How valuable is the living and active word of God to you? In Proverbs 7, Solomon says it should be the apple of our eye, that it should be written on our hearts, that we should call wisdom our sister and understanding our nearest of kin. The only other time this word for "nearest of kin" is used in scripture is in Ruth 2:1, which refers to Boaz, Ruth's kinsman-redeemer.

As such, it refers to a blood relative of the closest order. It is a derivative of the Hebrew word "to know," which has overtones of deep intimacy. God's Word and His Presence should be a leader's most prized possession and the thing most dear to them.

But why? Why should It be so highly prized?

Well, as you will see in the rest of Proverbs 7, it really is a lamp to our feet and a light to our path. In Proverbs 7, the author looks out of his window and notices a young man who he describes as being associated with the simple-minded, young, and devoid of understanding. This simple young man is wandering and happens upon a harlot who traps him with her crafty words. She's bold and boisterous, cunning and strategic, and he easily falls for her flattery since he lacks discernment. Solomon pens this analogy of what happens to this young man who lacks discernment and how easily he is led into temptation. You may not be easily led astray in this same exact way as this young man, but you need to identify and be aware of what easily leads you astray from the path of the Lord. Is it a certain relationship? Is it status, a title, or a position? Is it an internet site or maybe even your career? Is it a bottle or another substance? What is it that pulls you away? Don't shy away from allowing the Lord to shine His revelation light into those areas. Don't allow shame to keep you from bringing it to the surface and allowing the Lord to skim that stuff off like the dross from silver in the furnace. Our first step is to become aware of our vulnerable areas, allow the Lord to do His work, and then, like the author of Hebrews says, "Let us lay aside every weight and sin that so easily entangles us and let us run with endurance the race that is set before us."

When we allow the Living Word of God to wash over our hearts and minds, we have discernment. We can discern between good and evil and what is perceived to be good versus the things of God. We become aware in the moment of the subtle attacks of the enemy. It also allows us to take an offensive approach and not just play defense.

In Joshua 1, Moses has just died. Joshua has now assumed the role of leader for this nation which has been enslaved for over 400 years and has been living in the wilderness for the past 40 years. His role is to take this nation across the Jordan to possess the land promised to them. God tells Joshua, "This Book of The Law shall not depart out of your mouth, but you shall meditate on it day and night, that you may observe and do according to all that is written in it. For then *YOU* shall make *YOUR* way prosperous and then *YOU* shall deal wisely and have good success."

But what does it mean to meditate? It's not just about mindless repetition or idle contemplation. No, it's about something deeper, akin to a young lion growling over its prey. It carries a passionate intensity, an emotional connection. It's about hungering for the Word of God and seeking the revelation of His Truth. As Jesus proclaimed, those who yearn and thirst for righteousness are blessed, for their hunger will be satisfied.

One morning I was praying, and I heard the Lord say that His promises are the key to a transformed life. It's the promises found in His Word that wash over us to renew our minds. His Truths defeat anxiety, fear, and depression because there is freedom where the Presence of The Lord is. His Word is like life-giving water to our souls, and when we speak and release His promises, it's the same for those who hear. His Promises make up our offensive artillery to destroy lies, to demolish strongholds and every high thing that exalts itself against the Knowledge of Truth. But I must get *in* the Word for the Word to get *in* me.

Something incredible happens when the Living Word of God gets *in* you. When His Word moves from a set of words on a sheet of paper that we have memorized but makes its way into our hearts, it changes us, transforms us, and renews our minds. This is important for us as leaders because, without it, we are left wandering and find ourselves easily led astray, like the young man in Proverbs 7, who is gullible and easily deceived by the crafty words of the harlot.

As you grow in your leadership, many people will try to tell you what you should be doing to lead better and how to grow whatever you are leading. You should try this new tactic, this new trick. When we were growing our physical therapy and gym businesses, people often suggested a new marketing strategy or a new way to use social media. There was nothing necessarily wrong with their suggestions, but they were all attempts to make changes from the outside in instead of the inside out. The outside-in approach never results in long-term success because it has no foundation. When we allow the Word of the Lord to build our foundation, it changes the way we look at things. When we change how we look at things, the things we look at begin to change. We begin to see the world around us from a different perspective. When His Word shapes our hearts, we view the world around us from Heaven's perspective.

What scripture are you meditating on?

What do you feel like the Lord is revealing to you in this current season of your life?

Where do you see Him working right now?

Day 8

The Wealth of Nations

"You will find true success when you find me, for I have insight into wise plans that are designed just for you. I hold in my hands living understanding, courage, and strength. I empower kings to reign and rulers to make laws that are just." – Proverbs 8:14-15 TPT

I believe one of the lessons we must learn on our journey of maturity as leaders is understanding true humility. One of the things that are killing us as individual members of the body of Christ is not arrogance but false humility. We assume that if I begin to stand out and shine, that is arrogant and prideful when in reality, it is awareness. When we become aware of our unique gifts, talents, and abilities and begin to bring those forward to serve others, we are stepping into who God had in mind when He knit us together in the womb. We are each a unique expression of who He is and have been created in His image.

1 Peter 4:10-11 says, "Each of you should use whatever gift you have received to serve others, as faithful stewards of God's grace in its various forms. ¹¹If anyone speaks, they should do so as one who speaks the very words of God. If anyone serves, they should do so with the strength God provides, so that in all things God may be praised through Jesus Christ. To him be the glory and the power for ever and ever. Amen."

True humility is when we recognize the gifts we have been given and use those gifts to serve other people, all intending to bring glory to God. You must get your gifts into the game.

No one is served when we think small of ourselves or belittle ourselves. The moment we decide not to bring forward what we have been gifted, we not only hurt ourselves, but we rob the world of something truly incredible.

In the scripture above, Peter says we are to use whatever gifts we have received as faithful stewards. The word *steward* means someone entrusted by the owner to manage the owner's affairs. A steward is someone given authority and responsibility for a specific purpose. For example, the owner of a large farm would delegate trust and management to a leader who would take care of this large farm. This leader would be given the trust to make decisions, the authority to take action, and equipped with the resources required to be successful. A good leader would manage the farm well and would ultimately lead this farm to see an increase. It would be better when the leader handed back the authority to the owner than when he was given the authority. He would have stewarded well what was given to him.

The God of the universe loved you so much that He not only sent His Son, Jesus, as a way of salvation and intimate relationship but has graciously gifted each person with certain gifts, talents, and abilities. He has given us these gifts and the authority and responsibility to use these gifts. We can hide the gifts given to us or use them to prop ourselves up and serve our own selfish purposes. Both are examples of poor stewardship.

In Matthew 25:14-30, Jesus tells the parable of a man going on a long trip who entrusted his money to 3 different servants while he was gone. One servant was given 5 talents, another one was given 2, and the last one was given 1 talent, all according to their own ability. When the man returns, he gathers these 3 servants together to settle the accounts and to see how well they stewarded what was given to them. The first two put what was given to them to work and gained a double return for their master. The master replied, "Well done, good and faithful servant, you were faithful over a *few* things; I will make you *ruler* over many things." The last servant said that he knew his master was a hard man, reaping where he did not sow and gathering where he had not scattered. So, his response was fear, and he did not want to lose the talent he possessed, so he hid it in the ground. I'm sure this servant was shocked by the response he received from the master when the master said, "You wicked and lazy servant! You knew that I reap where I have not sown and gather where I have not scattered, so you ought to have deposited my money in the bank so at my coming, I would have received back my own with interest. Therefore, take the talent from him, and give it to him who has ten talents. For everyone who has, more will be given, and he will have abundance, but from him who does not have, even what he has will be taken away."

What is interesting to me about this entire parable is that the 3rd servant obviously did not know the master but only *knew of* the master. He probably had heard about the master or seen him from a distance, but he did not have a relationship with him. If his master was really how he described him, he would not have given the first two servants a greater reward or promotion. He would have kept everything to himself without giving recognition or honor.

When we draw near and spend time in the presence of the Living God, we begin to grasp His heart and begin to get a glimpse of how wide, how deep, how high, and just how long the love of Christ is, not just for other people, not just for the pastor of your church, or for Peter, Paul, or David, but for you too! When we capture that, we can then represent His heart well to those entrusted to our leadership. Isaiah 60 talks about how the abundance of the sea will be turned to you and the wealth of nations will come to you because of the light within you. We tend to view wealth and abundance as possessions and money; however, in the economy of Heaven, wealth is the soul of individuals. When we understand how much the Lord loves us, we can begin to love those within our circle of influence the way he loves us. We no longer see people as objects to be used or obstacles in our way, but as men and women created in the image of God with incredible potential that have the privilege to lead, serve, and pour into for a season of their lives.

One of the most important roles of a leader is to pull out the gifts, talents, and abilities of those they lead. Most people begin with the borrowed belief of someone else. They have someone in their lives, whether a coach, a teacher, a mother, father, grandparent, or employer, that comes along and says I see "this" in you, and I believe "this" is possible in your life. Every great person I have met or read about says the same thing; "She believed in me before I believed in me," or "He believed in me before I believed in me." We want to be that kind of leader for those we lead. We want to be belief makers.

When I was in the boy scouts, we had a saying we used when we went on campouts. We want to leave any and every territory we stay at better than we found it. I think we can pull that same thought over into the lane of leadership. We want anyone who ever comes underneath our leadership to be in a better position in life when they move on from our leadership than when they began. We can only lead from that place if we've spent precious time in the secret place with the Lord.

Do you know your strengths?

Up until now, how do you tend to view people?

What may need to change?

Day 9

"Heart Postured to Change the Course of History"

"So don't bother correcting a mocker; they will only hate you. But correct the wise, and they will love you. Instruct the wise, and they will be even wiser. Teach the righteous, and they will learn even more." – Proverbs 9:8-9

Having a teachable spirit is often the dividing line between wisdom and foolishness. Each interaction and each activity are opportunities to learn and an opportunity for feedback. It's making a mental shift from viewing events as simply good or bad to viewing them as lessons to be learned. Our experiences provide excellent learning opportunities, but only if we take the time to reflect and evaluate those experiences. When we take the time to reflect on our experiences, we allow the lessons to catch up with us. Failure is not fatal; there are only lessons to be learned if we have ears to hear. Each success leaves clues we can learn from and apply again for future opportunities. This is all a step into maturity and the application of wisdom.

Proverbs often mentions three words: knowledge, understanding, and wisdom, but what is the difference? Knowledge is an intellect of facts and information gained through education or experience. Understanding is knowing the *why* behind the information. Wisdom is taking all that knowledge and understanding and knowing when and how to apply it.

There is the wisdom of this world and the wisdom of man, but the Spirit-led leader has access to and should be led by a much higher level of wisdom, which is a gift from a good Father. This Wisdom is often much different from man's wisdom and plan.

In Mark 8:27-33, Jesus and His disciples are walking through the villages of Caesarea Philippi when He poses this question to them: "Who do people say that I am?" The people were obviously impressed with Jesus and held Him in high regard because some thought He was John the Baptist, some thought He was Elijah, and some thought of Him as one of the prophets. But then Jesus asked a more important question. "Who do *you* personally say that I am?" Peter responds with, "You are the Messiah!" This was revealed to Peter directly from God. So, Peter gets this amazing revelation from God that Jesus, this man right in front of him, is the long-awaited Messiah, and Jesus says, "Yes! You are correct."

Peter and the other disciples were all Jewish, and they grew up hearing about the Messiah; they heard the prophecies of reestablishing the throne of David, and they had a preconceived notion of what the Messiah was coming for. So, when Jesus begins to tell them plainly that He is about to be crucified and then raised to life three days later, it went against the belief system they were attached to. When Jesus began to talk about His upcoming death, Peter rebuked Him. We do not know what he said, but a rebuke is a sharp disapproval or criticism. Peter may have even used scripture to reprimand Jesus, but Jesus turned His back on Peter and made an interesting statement. He said to Peter, "Your heart is not set on God's plan but on man's." Peter was thinking nationalistically and not of God's bigger vision. Peter received Divine revelation but assigned man's meaning to it based on his own belief system.

That's the importance of posturing our hearts to be teachable and allowing our minds to be renewed and inwardly transformed by the Holy Spirit. When the Holy Spirit is allowed to do His work, He changes how we think, empowering us to discern God's will. As leaders, we run into problems, but we can go straight to God to see His thoughts on an issue or challenge. We can know His will on how to build our businesses. How about having the Creator of all things as your business partner?

Having a teachable and discerning spirit is a step toward maturity. Hebrews 5:14 TPT says, "But solid food is for the mature, whose spiritual senses perceive heavenly matters. And they have been adequately trained by what they've experienced to emerge with an understanding of the difference between what is truly excellent and what is evil and harmful."

As leaders who allow the Holy Spirit to renew our minds, we can discern His will and voice in situations that arise and the decisions we make. Our Father is not looking for a bunch of yes men and yes women or any "aye, aye captains" or servants. Jesus said I no longer call you servants but friends (John 15:15). He is looking for those with yielded hearts willing to be molded for a partnership that changes the course of history.

I will share a personal story with you to end today's devotion. One of the services I provide through my leadership business is one-on-one coaching. I had been coaching leaders for a few years when a friend recommended that I meet with an individual who was just starting out in coaching and wanted to open her own coaching practice. I honestly had no desire to meet with this leader, but I reluctantly agreed to meet out of respect for my friend. I was not really looking forward to meeting because my mindset was that this was not a wise use of my time, as I was in a very busy season of life. When we met, I realized how intelligent and capable this leader was. She impressed me with her credentials but mostly her intelligence. This was a trigger for me, because I have considered myself not very intelligent for as long as I can remember. When I meet extremely intelligent individuals, I become very unsure of myself and self-conscious. I thought this had been removed, but meeting with her brought this detrimental belief back to light.

I left our meeting having negative feelings toward her and being upset at her, but she gave me no reason to not like her. She was very kind and respectful, yet I was sitting in my truck mad at her, and I did not know why. Under my breath, I simply said, "Why am I mad at this lady when she has given me no reason to be mad?" Suddenly God spoke to me and said, "Do you want to know why?" I have found that when God asks you a question, you better consider your answer. So, sheepishly, I said yes. He then revealed to me that I was mad at her because I thought she was much smarter than I was, but not only that, because I believed she was smarter than I was, I also believed that she could serve my clients better than I could. I was honestly shocked at this truth. He then asked me a quick, direct question: "Do you want to serve people relying on your own intellect, or do you want my Spirit to lead you as you serve people?" I think I will rely on His Spirit.

Take a moment and reflect on the times in your life when you made decisions led by God. These may be decisions that you were unsure of, and even the leading did not make sense, but you listened and acted. Reflect on what was happening at the time and your emotions. Reflect on the outcome. Thank and praise Him for what He has done and is doing, and ask the Holy Spirit what He is saying about your direction right now. What is He teaching you in this season of life? What challenges or opportunities are you facing in this season? Ask Him what His thoughts and plans are.

As you and I lead and impact those we encounter, we can choose to be led by our own intellect, the intellect of the world, or the Spirit of Wisdom. Which will you choose?

Day 10

The Thumbprint You Leave Upon the World

"The reputation of the righteous becomes a sweet memorial to him, while the wicked life only leaves a rotten stench." – Proverbs 10:7 TPT

"While the wicked life only leaves a rotten stench" in the Hebrew manuscripts (this is according to the commentary in my Passion Translation Bible) and in the Aramaic reads, "the name of the wicked will be extinguished."

My wife knows that I like quotes, poems, and stories. She also knows that I try to be very aware of the legacy I am creating or, as a leader, the impact I am making in the lives of those I influence.

Not long ago, I received an unexpected invitation to speak at the funeral of my high school math teacher. Now, here's the thing: I hadn't seen or even talked to her in 20 years. But you know what's really surprising? Before she passed away, she specifically requested that I share something at her farewell.

Fast forward to the day of the funeral as I sat in my seat preparing for what I would say. I glanced at her obituary. I caught notice of two dates right at the top, and between these two dates, there was a space with a small dash. And let me tell you, that space held so much meaning. It hit me right then and there that we were all gathered to celebrate and remember that very space. That tiny gap symbolized my math teacher's tremendous impact on every one of our lives. It was a moment of reflection, gratitude, and recognition of her incredible influence.

Like my math teacher, you and I will have a space and a dash between two dates on our obituary. That dash represents your thumbprint or the mark you left on the hearts and minds of the individuals you cross paths with. Every single one of our lives crosses paths with history, but only a few will step into their calling to impact it.

When the children of Israel were about to cross over to take possession of the land that God had promised them generations before, they selected twelve leaders, one from each of the twelve tribes. These twelve leaders were selected and instructed to spy out the land and bring back a report of what they saw, along with some fruit of the land. Once these leaders returned, ten of the twelve gave into fear, while only two boldly stood up to step into the promise. The ten spread fear throughout the camp, saying, "We were as grasshoppers in our OWN sight and in their sight" (Numbers 13:33). However, the two bold leaders stood up to remind the people of the promise of God and said, "Let us go up at once and take possession, for we are well able to overcome" (Numbers 13:30). This bold stance for the truth and promise given by God caused the people to want to stone them to death! You know the rest of the story; because they gave into fear instead of the promise, they went back into the wilderness to wander for forty more years until this generation died off and a new generation of leaders rose to take possession of the promise. The only ones from this generation that were able to crossover were the two bold leaders, Joshua and Caleb.

No doubt you know or know of someone by the name of Joshua or by the name of Caleb, but do you know or have you heard of someone by the name of:

- Shammua
- Shaphat
- Igal
- Palti
- Gaddiel
- Gaddi
- Ammiel

- Sethur
- Nahbi
- Geuel

All twelve of these men were leaders. All twelve were selected by their tribes, which meant they had influence, had a good reputation among their peers, and were remembered for what they did and stood for. Joshua and Caleb were remembered for their bold stance, trusting in the promises of God. The other ten, you must dig to find their names, and they are remembered for enticing the crowd into fear, which led to forty years of making circles in a wilderness.

A.W. Tozer says, "God is looking for people through whom He can do the impossible-what a pity that we plan only the things we can do by ourselves."

It takes courage to lead, boldness to lead, and sometimes standing alone in the Truth. Ultimately, it takes being led by the Spirit. Spirit-led leadership is many times the opposite of our carnal thoughts and pays no regard to current circumstances and conditions. It's not the leader's might, it's not the leader's strength, but by His Spirit that we partner with Him to do the impossible. As leaders, we can do nothing of lasting value on our own.

What do you want to be known for?

What are you currently known for?

If there's a difference, what needs to change?

Day 11

Wise Counsel

"Without wise leadership, a nation falls; there's safety in having many advisors." – Proverbs 11:14 NLT

Who's in your inner circle? John Maxwell says that a leader's potential is determined by those closest to them. You have undoubtedly heard, "You are the average of the five people closest to you." So, who are those five people closest to you, and what does that currently say about your leadership potential? Do you have people in your life who will tell you the hard truth when that time comes but also will be there to support and help when you simply need a listening ear? Or do you have a bunch of "yes" men or women who never challenge you and are ok with you not stepping into your full potential?

There is a scripture in Proverbs that we often quote in our Christian circles: iron sharpens iron. That sounds great, and it sounds motivating, but the reality of that statement and the sharpening process is not a comfortable one. It's allowing someone else to get so close that they know the real you. The you with all your flaws, mistakes, and negative qualities, yet they still love you. They love you too much to leave you where you are. They listen and encourage when that is the need of the hour, they are present when the need arises, and they will challenge you on your BS (belief system) when they need to. They know that you, like themselves, are still in process, and it's in that process that each of you becomes better. Allowing people like that in our lives will help us step into our potential. We need friends like that, but that's also the type of friend we are called to be.

It truly is those closest to the leader that will determine their level of effectiveness. In 2 Chronicles 10, King Solomon has just died, and his son Rehoboam ascends to the throne as the next king of Israel. The leaders of Israel meet with Rehoboam and say that his father, King Solomon, was a hard master who put harsh labor and tax demands upon the people. These leaders requested a lighter load, and if their request was granted, they promised loyalty to his leadership. Rehoboam asked them to give him three days to consider their request. During those three days, Rehoboam sought out two different groups for wise counsel about this matter. The first group was the leaders, wise counsel, and older men who counseled his father, King Solomon. They recommended that Rehoboam treat the people well, treat them with kindness, do his best to please them, and ultimately serve the people. They said if he did this, the people would be loyal to him.

The second group from whom Rehoboam sought counsel was his buddies that he grew up with. Check out their recommendation to Rehoboam: "This is what you should say to those complainers. My little finger is thicker than my father's waist! My father laid on you a heavy yoke; I will make it even heavier. My father scourged you with whips; I will scourge you with scorpions." -2 Chronicles 10:10-11

Wow, how about that kind of advice? Well, Rehoboam chose the counsel of those closest to him and let the leaders of the people know that they only thought it was difficult when his father was king, and they should prepare to have their burdens multiplied and to serve him. This decision by Rehoboam led to the kingdom of Israel being split into the Northern Kingdom and the Southern Kingdom. Of the twelve tribes of Israel, only the tribes of Judah and Benjamin remained loyal to Rehoboam. Rehoboam's father prophetically spoke in Proverbs 11:14 that without wise counsel, a nation will fall. That's true for a nation, it's true for a business, and it's true for a family. We need wise Spirit-filled individuals in our lives.

If you have children, pay very close attention to whom they spend their time with. When you were growing up, your parents probably did not want you to hang out with certain individuals.

Why is that? Well, we know that whom our children spend time with affects the language they use, the attitudes they display, and the activities they are interested in. The question is, at what point and at what age is that no longer true? It is always true. I saw this all the time in the gyms we owned. One of the gyms we owned was a CrossFit gym. I would see individuals come in who did not work out. Still, after spending some time with the other athletes, they would begin to wear the typical workout clothes of a CrossFitter. They would buy CrossFit shoes, wrist wraps, and a specific jump rope and start eating paleo. The people they spent time with shaped their interests and influenced them. This is not a good or bad thing; it is something we must be mindful of as leaders who lead other leaders.

So, who is in your inner circle? Who are those five people closest to you? I want to encourage you to take some time to write down the names of those five people closest to you on a piece of paper. List them out and then reflect on what those relationships add to you. What are those relationships subtracting from you? Who do you need to spend more time with? Who do you need to spend less time with? Who do you need to stop spending time with? Does anyone need to be added?

Day 12

The Grass Appears to be Greener

"Thieves are jealous of each other's loot, but the Godly are well rooted and bear their own fruit." – Proverbs 12:12 NLT

As leaders, it is so easy to fall into the comparison trap. We compare our team to the other teams in the same industry. We compare our success or lack of success to other leaders. We see the superstars in the media, and we see all the perfect aspects of the lives of others posted on social media. We see the other business leaders making progress towards their goals, and we stop, stare, and compare, and we conclude that the adage "the grass is always greener on the other side" must be true. However, have you considered that the grass may only be greener on the other side because it receives better care? Maybe it's greener on the other side because somebody is taking the time to water it, feed it, and fertilize it, while we are standing there, propped up on the fence, comparing and admiring this beautifully manicured lawn while our own grass isn't receiving any attention. Because it is not receiving any attention or care, it's getting brown and crunchy, and weeds are spreading throughout.

In 2011, my wife and I decided to step out of our comfort zone and into the world of entrepreneurship. We dreamed about it for years and spent months planning and preparing. Our first business was going to be a physical therapy clinic. I had spent hours meticulously planning out this business and how we would financially make this shift for our family. As we were approaching the launch of our business, I drove around our city and found myself driving by all the other physical therapy clinics in the area. As I drove by their clinics, I noticed the names on the glass doors and on their signage, and following the names were their credentials. It was like looking at the alphabet. As I noticed the experience, accomplishments, and recognition of these other therapists, I began to compare myself to them, and the voice in my head began to tell me that I had no shot at competing with these amazing therapists. I saw all their accomplishments and saw that I had none. I saw their credentials and the alphabet after their names while I was "only" a physical therapy assistant. I knew their reputations, and they were not only some great therapists but also great people, while I was very much unknown.

I drove back home very down, and as I walked into our home, I told my wife exactly what I had just seen and that in no way would we be able to compete, so we should just pack it all up and not move forward on this dream because it will never work. My wife, seemingly unfazed by everything I told her, patiently listened as I complained and compared for several minutes. Once I finally stopped speaking, she nonchalantly said something very profound that changed my paradigm. What she said to me was only nine words. When I coach people in speaking, one of the things we talk about is whenever you're doing a speech, you want to keep it short, make it simple, and make it sizzle. That's exactly what my wife did when she used those nine words to literally snap me out of this comparison trap. All she said to me was, "But you know how to make people feel good." Those nine words changed my attitude and probably changed the trajectory of our lives.

It was at that moment that I realized what I was doing. I had been happily watering my own grass, but I just wanted to peek and see what the grass looked like on the other side. So, as I went to the fence, I noticed how bright green the grass was at these other locations. I started comparing myself to them, and I dropped my water hose and started to roll it up, but my wife snapped me out of it. Her nine words helped me understand that I have gifts, talents, and abilities and am unique. God has never made anyone exactly like me, and there will never be anyone with the exact gift mix I have or who thinks exactly like me. That sentence is true for me, it's true for all those awesome therapists I was comparing myself to, and that sentence is also 100% true for you. This world needs your gift, your talents, and your abilities. The moment you and I decide not to bring those forward, we hurt ourselves and rob the world of something truly incredible. You were made in the image of God. You are a unique expression of Him.

I do want to say that it is wise to observe what other successful leaders are doing so that we can learn from them. However, when we focus on how green their grass is and stop watering our own, or start measuring how large of a territory they have and stop putting out fertilizer on our own, we give our attention to what is not in our care.

In Proverbs 12:12, the root word for "loot" in this version is used metaphorically to indicate one who pursues the life of another to destroy it. The step beyond comparison is competing against; that says, for me to win, you must lose. This is a scarcity mindset. When we as leaders lead with a scarcity mindset, we begin to cut corners and relax on our values and integrity, changing how we interact with those we lead.

When we are rooted and grounded in focusing on serving with abundance, we begin to see optimistically and opportunistically. God is a God of abundance and a God of more than enough. As we are rooted in the Truth of who He is, that He is a good Father and that He has good and precious thoughts about you, so many good thoughts that they outnumber the grains of sand on the seashore, we no longer focus on competing; rather, we focus on creating. Psalms 139:17-18 (NLT) says, "How precious are your thoughts about me, O God. They cannot be numbered! I can't even count them; they outnumber the grains of sand! And when I wake up, you are still with me!"

He is for you and has great plans designed just for you. When we understand this truth, we no longer focus on competing. Instead, we focus on being His instrument to create, innovate, and change the world. Your winning does not take away from me, and my winning does not take away from you. I hope you will take some time to meditate on the truth that the Creator of the universe, who spoke all things into existence, has great thoughts toward you. He desires a deep, abiding, and intimate relationship with you.

What areas of your leadership are you comparing yourself or your ability to others?

Is there an area in your life you feel you are lacking in this current season? If so, ask the Holy Spirit to reveal those areas, then ask Him to reveal His truth about those areas.

Day 13

"A Team of Solutionaries"

"The one who guards his mouth [thinking before he speaks] protects his life;
The one who opens his lips wide [and chatters without thinking] comes to ruin." -Proverbs 13:3 (AMP)[4]

You've undoubtedly heard the phrase, "God has given us two ears and one mouth," so use that ratio when communicating. Listen twice as much as you speak. I think what we as leaders have a difficult time with is feeling like we always must have all the answers. Those we lead come to us with a challenge, and we feel the need to always provide the solution. When it comes to vision and direction, we feel like we must do it in isolation. When it comes to directing, we need to always tell people what to do, but if I am always telling the people I lead what to think, then I will never know what they are truly thinking. If I am always directing them on what to do, I will never know what they can do when empowered.

One of the jobs I had was working at a rehab hospital. One day, my leader came to me and asked me to lead an in-service for the hospital. This leader told me the topic and exactly what I should say during my delivery. I did not think much about this leadership approach because, honestly, it was the only type of

4   The Amplified® Bible, Copyright © 1954, 1958, 1962, 1964, 1965, 1987 by The Lockman Foundation. Used by permission. lockman.org

leadership I had experienced up until this point in my career. I took what my leader told me to share, and I delivered this in-service, and it fell flat; it was not any good. When it fell flat, I immediately began to point the finger at my leader and blame that leader for the failed in-service. I said to myself, "No one in this hospital cares anything about this particular topic, and who in the world even speaks like this!?" I cast the blame on someone else.

The next job was at an outpatient physical therapy clinic, and this leader was a very different leader named Tanny. He believed in equipping and empowering those he led. There was a doctor's office next to the physical therapy clinic where I worked, and each month, they held an in-service for diabetic patients in the community. Tanny came to me and asked me to speak at this monthly meeting. At this point, I was used to being told exactly what to do and exactly what to say, so I asked him, "What should the topic be on?" He responded, "Think about who you are speaking to and share what you think would be most beneficial to them." Shocked and stunned, I said, "Well, what in the world should I say?" Tanny replied, "Whatever you think they need to hear. Tell you what, I want you to think through it and share whatever you think would serve them. If you need some help, I'll be here, but I want you to own it and serve them." I thought through it and came up with something I thought would benefit them, which went well.

There were two things I learned from these two experiences. First, I learned that by being empowered and stretched outside my comfort zone, I found strength in communicating with groups I had previously not known about myself. Two, since he empowered me, if the speech fell flat, I had no one else to blame other than myself. I could not point the finger at anyone else. In the first scenario, because I was told exactly what to say and how it should be said, I did not accept personal responsibility for probably not being as prepared as I should have been or bringing as much energy as I could have.

When we equip and empower those we lead, we help them discover untapped areas of giftedness and empower them to take personal responsibility and ownership. We make this kind of transition by asking good questions. When I ask questions, I see their thoughts and opinions, and they may see something I do not see. They also get to give their input, making them feel like they are a part of the team. They feel like they are at the decision-making table, which encourages buy-in. When I ask good questions, I get to see their thinking and understanding, which helps me know when and where and how to step in and serve them well as a leader. When I ask questions, it helps to empower them to know how to think and not just what to think. I help them to begin to make leadership decisions. When I ask questions, I must posture my heart to hear and listen to what they say. Most leaders have a huge fault in hearing but not listening. I want to encourage you as a leader to posture your heart to truly listen when you ask questions. Also, when asking questions, we do not want to ask questions to prove a point or make our own case; we want to ask questions to truly understand. Most leaders listen with the intent to respond; some will posture themselves to listen to what is being said, but I want to encourage you to posture your heart to listen to the words behind the words—to watch the body language, to catch the tone of voice, and the words that are being said.

Research shows that in face-to-face communication, 55% of communication is body language, 38% is tone of voice, and only 7% is the words being spoken. To add value to those you lead, give them your time and your attention by listening to what their body language and tone of voice are saying along with their words.

I also want to help take some pressure off you as the leader. You do not always have to have all the answers, and you don't have to be perfect. People are not looking for stage perfection in a leader; they can't relate to that because no one is perfect. They want to see real people. Get your team to help you come up with solutions. Develop and empower a team of solutionaries by asking good questions. Jesus demonstrated this in the feeding of the 5000.

In John 6, Jesus had been teaching the crowds all day, and it was beginning to get late in the evening. He looks to Philip and asks him, "Where can we buy bread to feed all these people?"

Scripture then says He asked Phillip this to test him because He already knew what He was going to do. What!? Why would Jesus ask a question He already knew the answer to? Remember, Jesus knew that His ministry on earth would be short, and He was working to equip His disciples to carry on the gospel once He ascended. He was equipping them to begin thinking with a Kingdom mindset. They were facing the challenge of what they would do with all these people, who were probably hungry. They could tell them it was time to go home because the challenge of feeding all these people seemed impossible. They could run to the market and attempt to buy some bread with the amount of money they had and try to feed as many as they could, or they could begin to think from Heaven's standpoint to solve the problem. Jesus wanted His disciples to look to Him for solutions to problems. He still desires us to look to Him in all our circumstances.

Let me share with you a perspective that all of us, as Kingdom-minded leaders of our generation, should adopt when confronted with challenges and opportunities. You see, we have a choice. We can either rely on our limited human thinking or turn to the wisdom of this world for solutions. But here's the exciting part: we also have the option to offer Heavenly solutions to our earthly problems. How? By seeking guidance from the Holy Spirit Himself. He holds the answers we need; all we have to do is ask. It's a powerful way to approach life's hurdles and make a lasting impact.

We should be the wisest people on the planet. We should be coming up with solutions to the world's problems because we have the Spirit of the Living God within us. We have the mind of Christ. We simply come to Him with humble hearts and ask. Seek, and you will find, knock and the door will be opened, ask, and you will receive.

Do you tend to lean more toward telling or asking questions?

Do you tend to ask questions to prove a point or to truly understand?

What may need to change or improve in how you listen?

Day 14

The Only Clean Stable is an Empty One

"Without oxen a stable stays clean, but you need a strong ox for a large harvest." – Proverbs 14:4 NLT

The farmer with a dream of a large harvest had to have a few animals. The problem with having a few animals is that they need to be fed, they need to be watered, and there would need to be a level of cleaning up after their messes to keep them healthy. So, the farmer has a choice: give up the dream, or decide to go to work and take care of his team.

There are a couple of sayings in leadership, "If you have a big dream, then you better have a big team," and "If you can accomplish your dream on your own, then you are not dreaming big enough." When you lead a team of equipped and empowered people, there is a multiplication that kicks in. When we empower and equip those we lead, it is not growth by addition; it is growth and impact by multiplication. However, fully equipping and empowering those we lead is an up-close process. Many leaders fear getting close to those they lead out of fear of the "what ifs." What if I become too close and leave myself open to hurt, or they abuse our relationship? What if I do all the work to train them, and then they leave? The rebuttal question is, "What if you don't work to train them up, and they stay?"

Sometimes, we also question, "What if they mess up or make a major mistake?" We all sometimes mess up, and we as leaders have made major mistakes. In fact, at some point, we have probably messed up on the very thing we are fearful of handing off. When we ask this question, we assume that we have not and will not make a mistake ourselves. If we do not hand off by equipping someone else, we will always be doing that task, and we will be a cap on our team and on the potential of those we lead.

When we choose to keep the individuals we lead at a distance, they may not hurt us, but they cannot fully help us, either. If you get close to those you lead, will someone abuse you, use you, or accuse you? Probably, but it's only by leading people up close that life is impacted and great work is accomplished. Choose to get to know your people. Choose to let your people get to know you. Impact only happens at close range.

People are often difficult, but I love what Bob Goff says: "Love difficult people. You are one of them." Jesus is our greatest example of leadership. He took twelve common men, not the religious scholars of the day, but men with hearts postured to be led by Him. In Luke 9, Jesus calls the twelve together and gives them power and authority over all demons and authority to heal diseases. In Luke 10, He sends out seventy to do the same thing. These people had potential but also had the potential to make mistakes. If you read scripture, they competed against one another to see who would be the greatest; they often doubted and had little faith, and they wanted to call down fire from Heaven to consume those that opposed and insulted them. Yet it was these people that Jesus got close to, He did life with, He demonstrated, He "coached" and "mentored" them, and He empowered them to advance His Kingdom.

As Jesus ascended into Heaven, He said all authority on Heaven and earth has been given to me; go therefore and make disciples of all nations. Take my authority as my representatives from Heaven and make the place you were sent to look like where you were sent from. That was given to His disciples but also to mistake-prone men and women like you and me when we gave our "yes" to Jesus Christ as our Lord and Savior. The great thing is we are sealed with His Spirit and are led by His Spirit, so we are not left alone.

When you partner with God to do incredible things to advance the Kingdom, there will probably be some things to clean up because we shake the status quo of culture. The moment you choose to build great people as a leader, you will undoubtedly have some mistakes to clean up. I will tell you upfront that it will not be easy, and you may have a mess or two or even hundreds to clean up, but it will be worth it!

How willing are you to do the clean-up work that comes from developing something great and from developing great people?

Is there anything that needs to change in your perspective on leading into greatness?

Day 15

Humility Leads to Honor

"The fear of the Lord is what wisdom teaches, and humility comes before honor." – Proverbs 15:33 CSB[5]

The reverential awe, wonder, and worship of God is the very beginning of true wisdom. It is amazing to think that with God's spoken word, all of creation came into existence. You can check out images taken from space showing the vastness of the galaxies and universe. You can grab a microscope to check the tiniest of particles, and you will see life. In my college anatomy and physiology class, I was awestruck by how intricately the internal systems and organs of our body operate and work together. I found it fascinating that if just one single chromosome is out of place, how that affects the body. Our God deserves all of our praise and all of our worship. Our awe of Him should never become common or ordinary. When we humble ourselves under His leadership, honor comes.

I think we as leaders, and culture in general, have a hard time understanding both of those terms: honor and humility. Our culture says I deserve to be honored because of who I am, but the Kingdom aligns more with, "I know who I am and whose I am; therefore, I honor you." Humility is not making ourselves out to be less than others. That's false humility. It recognizes

---

5   Scripture quotations marked CSB are taken from The Christian Standard Bible. Copyright © 2017 by Holman Bible Publishers. Used by permission. Christian Standard Bible®, and CSB® are federally registered trademarks of Holman Bible Publishers, all rights reserved.

who I am in Christ Jesus as a son/daughter in the Kingdom of God. I have been redeemed and adopted into a royal family. True humility is where I recognize the talents, gifts, and abilities that I have been given, and I use those gifts, talents, and abilities to serve others for His glory alone and not mine. Anything that points back to me is not true humility. Arrogance says, "Look at me, look at me, see what I did." False humility says, "Oh, woe is me, woe is me." But "look at me, look at me" and "Oh, woe is me, woe is me" both point back to me.

True humility is not thinking less of myself but of myself less. It's recognized that I am gifted, talented, and unique, that there has never been anyone exactly like me. There never will be anyone exactly like me. I am a unique expression of Him. So, I use the gifts that He has given to me to serve other people. That exact statement is true for you, and it is true for those you lead as well.

We have all been born with natural abilities. When we receive Jesus as Lord and Savior, we are sealed with His Spirit, and the Holy Spirit also distributes spiritual gifts. Today's devotion regards our natural abilities. As we lead, we know that to steward well the abilities we have been gifted, we need to be intentional about our growth and development. We also know that growth only occurs outside of our comfort zone. So, we want to consistently be out of our comfort zone but never out of our strength zone. That's the area of your natural giftings, and staying in those strength zones allows you to serve others at a higher level. Besides, we are not any good in our areas of weakness. We want to improve our strengths and shore up our weaknesses through other people who possess those strengths that we lack.

You may be asking, "Shouldn't I focus on improving my weaknesses so that I'm well-rounded?" My answer to that question is no, and here is why. On a scale of 1-10, let's just say that I am a 2 when it comes to administrative tasks. I could focus on improving this weakness by attending courses, seminars, or webinars. I could hire coaches and mentors to help me improve; over time, I could see that 2 improve to a 5. That's a pretty good improvement, but 5 is average. It's mediocre. I do not want to be mediocre at anything. The people you and I lead deserve better than an average leader; they deserve an exceptional one. People do not pay, seek out, or recommend average. We do not go back to work on Mondays and tell everyone about the average meal we had at the average restaurant. People deserve and are looking for the exceptional.

Now let's say, on a scale of 1-10, that when it comes to communicating or public speaking, I'm a 6, which is a strength of mine. I could focus on improving this strength by attending courses, seminars, webinars, and reading books. I could hire a coach or mentor, etc., and I would see that strength improve over time. Maybe that strength improves from a 6 to an 8 or even a 9; now, we are talking world-class. People are looking for world-class. They gladly pay for world-class. They take note of excellence, and as ambassadors of our Lord Jesus, we should do all things with excellence. We should carry ourselves with excellence to the point that people take note and say there is something different about us and want to know what it is.

In 1 Kings 10, the Queen of Sheba visits King Solomon. King Solomon's reputation for wisdom and wealth had extended throughout the world, and many kings and queens came to meet with him. The Queen of Sheba had heard about his fame and said to herself, "I need to go check this out." So, she goes to meet with King Solomon. Scripture says she spoke to him about everything on her mind, and nothing was too difficult for Solomon to answer or explain to her. But then she saw how his table was set, how his servants were dressed, and how they carried themselves; it took her breath away. It was excellence in the details and small things that caused a queen to gasp and respond with, "Not even half had been told to me."

We should be leaders representing the King of kings in everything we do and do it with such excellence that it causes the world to gasp.

Often, once we become aware of our gifts and begin to operate in them, we have this false belief that it is arrogance. It is not arrogance; it is awareness. The moment we hold back and settle for something less and do not bring those gifts to light because of false humility, then that is rebellion against the gifts that God has freely given. True humility recognizes where we're naturally strong and uses those areas to serve others to bring glory to God! At the same time, we need to be open and willing wholeheartedly to give Him a loud yes when the Holy Spirit asks to lead us from a place of weakness.

What are your natural strengths? What do you do well? What are some of the things people often compliment you on? Those are clues.

Ask the Holy Spirit right now where He wants to use you. Spend time with Him and journal what He says.

Day 16

In a Moment of Decision

"Commit your work to The Lord and your thoughts will be established." -Proverbs 16:3 NKJV

One of the key skill sets in being a great leader is decision-making. In fact, successful leaders have a habit concerning decision-making. They have the habit of making decisions quickly and changing their minds slowly. Unsuccessful leaders also have a habit around decision-making; they make decisions slowly and change their minds quickly. I love what President Theodore Roosevelt said: "In any moment of decision, the best thing you can do is the right thing, the next best thing is the wrong thing, and the worst thing you can do is nothing."

When we receive the facts, leaders must make a decision. A visionary person may be able to see, but a leader must decide. So, how do we as leaders make quick decisions when those decisions are often being made under pressure?

Before studying leaders and gaining experience, I would gather all the people I know, ask for their opinions, and make decisions based on a consensus. Consensus of opinion is not a strategy for success for a leader in making decisions.

To make good decisions and to make those decisions quickly while under pressure, two things must be concrete before the moment of decision arrives.

1. The big picture. This is your overall vision and direction in which you and/or your team are going.
2. Core values. These are your non-negotiables, and they

must be determined upfront.

Knowing where we are going and what we value allows us to make better decisions more quickly.

I know many times, as Kingdom-minded leaders, we can get caught up in the cycle of "But is this God's will for my life?" and "I just want to make sure that I am leading in alignment with God's will." I get that, but if we look at our key verse in Proverbs today, it says that if we commit our work or whatever we do to the Lord, then our thoughts will be established. Interestingly, when we commit to the Lord, something supernaturally happens in our thought life. If I commit to Him to the depth of my heart the work I do, then he takes on the task of aligning my thoughts with His will. To make quick, good decisions, we must have our vision and values determined, but it begins with a commitment. Once that commitment is made, He will establish our thoughts so that the vision we come up with and the values we hold fast to align with His.

I want to look at two leaders in the same scenario who made different decisions. In Matthew 27, Judas plotted with the Jewish leaders to have Jesus killed. Jesus is brought before the governor at that time, Pilate, for questioning. During this illegal questioning, the Jewish leaders throw out all these allegations while Jesus just stands and listens. Pilate is observing all of this and is gathering some details but is amazed that Jesus says absolutely nothing. He knows internally that the Jewish leaders only brought Jesus to him because they were envious of Him (vs.18), but they are also very passionate and angry with their intent. Pilate knows that this week is a festival week, and there are many visitors to the city. He also knows that if chaos ensues, he will be held responsible. His wife even comes to advise him not to have anything to do with Jesus because of a dream that she had. In a moment of decision while under extreme pressure, Pilate gives in to consensus of opinion.

On the other hand, Jesus was hanging on a wooden cross as the Son of God, God in the flesh, and people were shouting insults at Him. They said, "He saved others, but He cannot save Himself," "If He is the Son of God, come down so we can believe in Him" (vs. 42). "If God really cares for Him, He could deliver Him." (vs. 43) Just for a moment, consider the pressure. Put yourself in Jesus' situation just for a moment. You are in extreme pain, and you could make it go away with a spoken word. People are questioning your identity and tempting you to do something you could easily do. But Jesus had a much bigger vision in mind: His decision to stay obedient to where He was would pave the way for the salvation of billions. He kept in mind the value of a deep relationship with you to the point He decided to stay put. WOW!

Do you know your vision, and can you clearly articulate it?

What are your non-negotiables?

Day 17

Pressure Creates Diamonds

"The crucible for silver and the furnace for gold, but the LORD tests hearts." -Proverbs 17:3 NIV[6]

The crucible for silver and the furnace for gold, but people are tested by their praise. – Proverbs 27:21 NIV

Gold and silver are heated until they become a liquid which causes the impurities, called dross, to rise to the top. The dross is then removed to purify the gold or silver. Throughout scripture and here in Proverbs 17:3, it says the Lord tests our hearts. Why would He do that, and what does it mean to test our hearts? He tests our hearts not to judge and condemn us but to bring to the surface some things He wants to remove. The thing about precious metals like silver and gold is that they are simply objects and have no choice but to go through the refining process.

On the other hand, we have been blessed with free will; we can receive and submit to the refining process, resist the process, complain about it, make excuses, or be unwilling to learn the lessons offered through the process. We can say *why me* or complain, or we can allow what's being revealed to become real to us and allow a loving Father to walk us through the process of purifying our hearts. The process refines us and draws us into

---

6   Scripture quotations marked NIV are taken from THE HOLY BIBLE, NEW INTERNATIONAL VERSION®, NIV® Copyright © 1973, 1978, 1984, 2011 by Biblica, Inc.® Used by permission. All rights reserved worldwide.

a deeper relationship with Him.

Proverbs 24:10 says that if you faint in your day of adversity, your strength is small. As a leader, you were made to do hard things; if there were no challenges or difficulties, then there would be no need for a leader. But how do you respond when adversity strikes? What is your natural response? Adversity, trials, and difficulties are all revelators. They reveal what's deep within. In this proverb, if our response is to faint or to slack, which means to procrastinate or to be slow in doing what needs to be done, then our strength is small.

Interestingly, the word for *small* in this verse means to constrict or limit the flow. Kind of like allowing traffic to flow in only one direction. So, when tough times hit, which they hit us all at some point, what's our typical response? If, in a day of deep intense difficulty, our response is to pull away, procrastinate, and depend on our own strength and wisdom, then we are limiting the flow of God's strength and wisdom. Our other option is to look to Him.

> *"Give your burdens to The Lord, and He will take care of you. He will not permit the godly to slip and fall."*
> *-Psalm 55:22.*

> *"Give all your worries and cares to God, for He cares about you." -1 Peter 5:7.*

When adversity strikes, people either become bitter or choose to get better. They either depend upon themselves or look to God for His love and infinite wisdom. Adversity will destroy superficial faith, but it strengthens real faith by causing believing leaders to dig their roots deeper into God. It's never fun to look at those moments of failure and shine a light on the mistakes, the poor decisions, or our inability to measure up to the moment. However, those moments offer tremendous lessons and a measure of wisdom we never would have received, but we have a decision to make.

We can choose to get bitter and sad and never think about the moment again because it is just too painful or embarrassing, or we can determine within us that "I will grow from this; I choose to look and dig to find the nuggets of wisdom because I have this burning desire to be better." In my experience, I have come to understand that experience is not the greatest teacher, but evaluated experience is. When we take the time to evaluate our experiences, we allow the lessons within those experiences to catch up with us. A key that all the greats know is that failure is not the enemy. Failing to learn the lesson or falling and staying down is the enemy.

The two proverbs we have as our key verses offer an interesting contrast. One refers to the refining process we go through during the valleys and what is revealed in those moments, but that is not the only way character is revealed. In Proverbs 27:21, character is revealed by giving a leader power and giving them praise. Abraham Lincoln said, "Nearly all men can stand adversity, but if you want to test a man's character, give him power."

However, what truly impresses me are the athletes who maintain a composed demeanor, as if they've been there before and have the unwavering expectation that they will achieve greatness again. You see, for them, it's not just a one-time occurrence. It's ingrained in their very being; it's who they are and what they do. These individuals exemplify true champions.

What sets these true champions apart is their unwavering confidence. They don't feel the need to prove their worth to others. They don't seek validation or attention by making grand announcements or creating a scene. Instead, their actions, work ethic, interactions with others, and the consistent results they produce speak volumes on their behalf.

In contrast, those who strive to constantly prove themselves or impress others reveal a lack of true championship. Their identity is not firmly rooted in their abilities but rather in the opinions and validation of others. True champions, on the other hand, find their identity in their very essence, in their character and dedication to their craft. They let their actions and results do the talking, for their accomplishments validate their status without needing external affirmation.

How we receive praise reveals where, what, and who we get our identity from.

The key to leading well and walking these two proverbs out

is rooted in Who we get our identity from. If we know and understand in our hearts that we are sons and daughters of the King, it changes the way we respond to the highs and the lows. It changes how we react to adversity and moments of public recognition. You will no doubt face challenging times occasionally, but as you continue to grow and lead others at a high level, you will be given opportunities to be recognized.

The challenges we face, our failures, and even our response to praise bring what's deep within to the surface. Like the dross that rises to the surface, we can choose to allow God to skim these imperfections out of our lives, or we can allow the impurities to return to the depths of our hearts. These moments are simply opportunities for awareness. Once I am aware of something, I can do something about it. That's why we say in leadership that experience is not the greatest teacher, but evaluated experience is. When we evaluate our experiences, we take the time to become aware of the lessons offered by our experiences.

Spend a few minutes and ask the Holy Spirit what He loves about you.

Spend a few minutes and ask the Holy Spirit what areas in your character He would like you to become aware of.

Day 18

Having the Power of Life and Death

"Death and life are in the power of the tongue, and those who love it will eat its fruit." – Proverbs 18:21 (ESV)[7]

There is power in the spoken words of a leader. Our words are like seeds sown into the soil of other people's lives. They never remain neutral. They yield a harvest, either life or death, building people up or tearing them down, constructive or destructive.

A retired teacher reached out to me the other day and shared an experiment she used to do with her middle school classroom. The experiment showed the impact of bullying and the power of our words. The students took two identical plants and set them on the windowsill. They watered them at the same time and with the same amount, and they ensured the two plants had the same amount of sunlight. The only difference was that the students were instructed to speak negative words to one and positive and affirming words to the other one. As the students passed by the one plant, they would say things like, *you will never grow; you are the ugliest plant; your leaves will turn brown; you are worthless,* etc. As they passed by the other one, they would say things like, *you are strong, you are beautiful,* etc. She told me

---

7 "Scripture quotations are from the ESV® Bible (The Holy Bible, English Standard Version®), copyright © 2001 by Crossway, a publishing ministry of Good News Publishers. Used by permission. All rights reserved. The ESV text may not be quoted in any publication made available to the public by a Creative Commons license. The ESV may not be translated in whole or in part into any other language."

that within 30 days, there was a noticeable difference between the two plants. The negative plant was droopy, with leaves turning brown, while the positive plant was vibrant, green, and healthy. Our words have power, and the words of a leader carry extra weight because, as a leader, you have influence.

Moses made a plea and drew a line in the sand for the children of Israel in Deuteronomy 30. He spoke to them, saying, "Now listen! Today I am giving you a choice between life and death, between prosperity and disaster. I call heaven and earth to witness against you today, that I have set before you life and death, the blessing and the curse. So choose life." The line was drawn in the sand to be committed to God or not. The line is drawn in the sand for us as leaders as well, including how we will commit to using the power of the words we speak, to speak life or death.

As leaders, we want to see the gold in other people's lives, call it out, and expect its fruit. It takes zero talent and zero skill to call out the dirt in other people's lives. Anyone can do that. It takes a leader with eyes and a heart of compassionate desire to see, recognize, and call out the potential in the lives of others. When I talk about this within companies and teams, occasionally, someone will say, "Cory, you're overlooking their faults and mistakes." It's not that I am overlooking those faults because we will eventually address those things along the way. However, what I have found is that most people are well aware of the dirt and the mistakes in their lives because they've been told about them many times, but they've never had anyone bold enough to introduce them to their potential.

A diamond mine is not laced floor to ceiling with visible diamonds, but all that is seen is the dirt. You have to dig through the dirt to mine out the diamonds. People are often the same way. Almost all the great people I have met or read about have a story with a transition moment that sounds alike — "someone believed in me before I believed in me." We want to be leaders who do that for the individuals we lead and introduce people to their potential.

There's a powerful quote by Johann Wolfgang von Goethe that says, "If you treat an individual as he is, he will remain how he is. But if you treat him as if he were what he ought to be and could be, he will become what he ought to be and could be." This statement holds so much truth regarding our interactions with others. When we choose to speak and treat people based solely on their circumstances, we can't expect them to change or experience transformation. However, when we speak life into their lives, recognizing and acknowledging the incredible potential we see in them, it ignites a spark of confidence within them. It opens up a world of possibilities, allowing them to dream and become someone they may have never envisioned.

One simple way to put this into practice is by catching people doing something right and letting them know about it. We often tend to focus on pointing out faults and mistakes. While correcting and guiding are important, we sometimes overlook the moments when individuals do things correctly. We encourage them to repeat those positive actions by recognizing and acknowledging those moments.

Another effective approach is to call out and highlight the strengths and gifts we see in others. I recently heard a pastor share an insightful story about their church organization with multiple campuses. Some campuses outperformed others, and they discovered the key difference upon investigation. The successful campuses had one thing in common—they saw the talents in their volunteers and team members and made sure to let them know. As leaders, we often recognize potential and talent in others, but we forget to vocalize it. Take the time to see and speak out loud about the strengths and gifts you observe in those you lead.

Lastly, let's not forget that we have the Spirit of God within us. We have the Holy Spirit and the mind of Christ, enabling us to speak prophetically into the lives of those we lead, to speak in alignment with Heaven's perspective about that individual and how God sees them. You can even ask the Holy Spirit directly, 'What is your favorite thing about this person?' and then listen attentively to His response. Remember, every single person, regardless of whether they believe in Jesus Christ or not, was created in the image of God and crafted on purpose for a purpose.

God does not make mistakes, and He certainly doesn't create junk. So, let's seek His viewpoint on each individual and speak accordingly.

Up until now, have your words been more life-giving or life-taking?

What may need to change in your use of words?

Day 19

"When the Blessing Becomes a Curse"

"Lazy people sleep soundly, but idleness leaves them hungry." -Proverbs 19:15 (NLT)

One of the many blessings found throughout the precious living Word of God is rest. In fact, God Himself worked six days and created all things then He rested. Scripture says He rested; He did not quit. In John 5:17, the Pharisees were mad at Jesus because He healed a man on the Sabbath. Jesus tells them, "My Father has been working until now, and I work too."

There is a season of rest, and there are cycles where we should rest. God provided us with an example for us to work but also take our rest. Our society often wears hard work as a badge of honor and uses the phrase, "I'm just busy," to declare to the world just how in-demand our time is. I recently spoke to a friend, and he shared with me that for the longest time, he took pride that no one else worked as hard and did not put in nearly the number of hours as he did. It was an area of pride for him until he noticed others on his team were not working nearly as many hours or as hard as him, yet they were much more productive. God encourages times and seasons of rest so we are rejuvenated and mentally, physically, and spiritually refreshed. Ultimately, He says to rest in Him, meaning not to be anxious about anything but to trust in Him. He also means to take seasons and times for a sabbath break.

Our enemy is not a creator; he's an imitator and a corrupter. He can take something that God made and called good and can twist it to be evil. In Ezekiel 16:49, one of the sins of Sodom was idleness or laziness. Idleness can happen when we allow a season intended for rest to extend beyond the desired time frame of God and become a lifestyle. Idleness includes simply being lazy but implies being busy doing unimportant things. As leaders, we know that not all activity equals accomplishment. In 2 Thessalonians 3:11-12, Paul tells the church that they have some who aren't doing anything and are simply busybodies. So, he encourages them to do their work quietly and to earn a living. God works through us but can't if our hands are idle. Work is good, but it should be balanced with knowing when to pause.

In Luke 19, Jesus tells a parable about the ten minas. In the parable, a man of noble birth was going away to be appointed king and gave 10 of his servants 10 minas to be put to work. I find it very interesting that the ones found faithful with what little they had been entrusted were given more responsibility. They were faithful with a very small matter, so they were given authority and responsibility over cities. Did you catch that? They were faithful to the work they had been entrusted with, and their reward for a job well done was more work. Work is a good thing. Being responsible and doing all that you do as you would do for the Lord Himself is a good thing. Rest is a good thing. But extended rest beyond its intended season and reason is not. That's being lazy and idle.

When I think of the word idle, I think back to my grandmother. She had this old lawn mower and would ask me to mow the yard for her. She said when you crank up the mower, you must let it idle a bit for it to work properly. The mower was working, and the engine was running, but it was not going anywhere. It was functioning, but it was not operating in its function. It was not doing the work it was designed to do, mowing the yard, but it sounded like it was.

Idleness can be described as not doing anything and sitting still. It could also be described as busy not doing things you should be doing, which often leads to doing what you should not be doing.

> *"In the spring, at the time when kings go off to war,*
> *David sent Joab out with the king's men and the whole*

Israelite army. They destroyed the Ammonites and besieged Rabbah. But David remained in Jerusalem."
-2 Samuel 11:1

This Scripture says King David decided to stay home when he should have gone to war. He was busy not doing what he should have been doing, which led him to do what he should not have done. A few verses later, David is on the rooftop, notices a beautiful lady bathing, and sends for her. This decision led to David committing adultery and then killing Bathsheba's husband, Uriah, one of David's thirty mighty men.

A popular quote in the leadership/personal growth space says if you do not take control of your calendar, someone else will. This means that your time, if not intentionally taken over, will always be filled, sometimes with things you'd rather not be doing. But what would it look like if we allowed a specific Someone to take over our calendar? I mean, He is a good Father; He does have a good plan for your life, so what if we asked Him to fill our day?

I just want to end today with three really practical time-maximizing tools that I use. I hope this helps you as you lead the most difficult persona you will ever lead—yourself.

Tool number 1: The Pareto principle, or the 80/20 rule, states that for many events, roughly 80% of the effects come from 20% of the causes. Basically, if I have ten tasks for the day and if I have them numbered from number one most important to number ten least important, then the top 2 would give me 80% of my production.

Tool number 2: The three R's. I learned this from John Maxwell; it has been a game-changer. I list out all my responsibilities or tasks and then ask three questions.

1. Is this task **required** of me? These are the tasks that only you can do and cannot be delegated to someone else.
2. Does this give me a good **return** on my time? Is this a task that I am good at? Is this in my strength zone?
3. Is this task **rewarding**? Life is too short not to enjoy it. We are most productive when we are doing the things we truly enjoy. Another way to say it: what task do you enjoy

so much that you would do it for free?

I challenge you to reflect on your previous 7 days, find 3-5 wins during that time frame, then look at all the tasks you did and take those tasks through the 3 R's. What needs to change? What do you need to do more of? What do you need to do less of?

Day 20

Becoming A Leader Worth Following Through the Process

"An inheritance gained hastily at the beginning will not be blessed at the end." - Proverbs 20:21 NKJV

Ahh, the process! As a leader with a vision, big dreams and plans, I know you want the results to happen yesterday. We want our successes to happen overnight and desire to become the leader who achieves great things right now. The process we truly want is the microwave process when the leader who has staying power has been developed in the crockpot. John Maxwell says that leadership does not happen in a day, but it does happen daily. Becoming the type of leader who can say "follow me" begins with what we choose to do day in and day out. It's the daily process of becoming a leader worth following.

No doubt you have heard about lottery winners who became multi-millionaires overnight, but then, just a few short years later, they not only have lost it all but are in extreme debt. We wonder, how in the world could something like that happen? Well, it happens because those individuals did not develop the habits of being a millionaire. They did not go through the process of learning how to think, manage, and steward money well. When they were instantly handed large sums of money, their lack of development in this area was magnified. They were millionaires, but they had not *become* millionaires.

This happens to leaders when the opportunity exceeds the development in character. In the proverb above, the inheritance gained with haste is not blessed because the one getting it has not been equipped to handle it wisely. Through the process, we develop habits, skills, wisdom, and, ultimately, the strength of character.

In Genesis chapters 37-50, there is a young man named Joseph. He's 17 years old and has a call on his life to do something great. He probably felt it at an early age and had some kind of internal knowing. You, as a leader, know exactly what I mean. There's this burning desire somewhere deep down inside you, something deep down that says you were made for greatness. Well, Joseph begins to have some dreams of leadership, in particular, leading his family. But because of his arrogance and immaturity, he begins to let his older brothers and family know about this dream. His older brothers, being jealous of him, decided to just get rid of him by throwing him into a pit and then selling him into slavery.

It took another thirteen years in slavery, in prison, and going through trials, disappointments, and accusations before he stood before Pharaoh in the palace, where he ultimately became second in command. This was what he dreamed about. But between the pit and the palace was the process.

The process is what matured and developed this immature young man into a wise leader on the world's stage, allowing him to lead with wisdom during a world crisis. However, we like to skip the process and get right to the dream. We want to microwave our way to the end result, but it's that microwaved process that causes us to have no staying power because the strength of character has not been developed when we microwave it. It's in the process where we develop the strength of character; it's only in the testing that the development of our character is revealed. That's when the depth of our character surfaces. Anyone can have a good attitude and character when things are going good and when things are going our way. When faced with adversity, we have a choice: will I become bitter, or will I get better? I want to encourage you to choose the latter. I want to encourage you, to instill courage into you, so that courage is available when those moments of adversity come. You will have the character to stand the test and the trials and can become the leader that other people willfully follow because of who you are and what you represent.

I think we have this expectation that everything should come easily and quickly and that we should have a life of ease, but a life of ease does not equip and strengthen us. It doesn't develop the character muscle within us. Only when we face challenges and have the opportunity to choose our character does our true character begin to develop. So, in this process of growth, we are developed, and this process comes in phases. There are four phases that you'll go through in your growth journey as a leader:

1. I don't know what I don't know.
2. I know what I don't know.
3. I know and grow, and it starts to show.
4. I simply go because I know.

The first phase is *I don't know what I don't know*. This is when you are starting out, and there are some things you simply do not know yet. When we started our businesses, my wife and I did not know anything about operating a business, nor did we grow up in a family where entrepreneurship or business was discussed. My mom loved us and did the best she could, but her philosophy was more like going to school, getting a good degree, getting a good job, and staying *there for 87 years*. However, that was not appealing to me at all because I had this entrepreneurial spirit within me. When we launched our business, I had no idea what in the world we were doing. I just knew we wanted to do it, and I knew we wanted to make an impact. We had this vision, but how to make this vision a reality was unknown to me. So, I did the one thing I knew to do: go to my friend Google. Google helped us out a lot in those first few months and years because there were things that I just did not know. That's true for you as well. The dream that you've got, that thing inside of you, you know it's there, but there are many things about making it a reality that you are unaware of now.

The second phase is *I know what I do not know*. This is where I become aware of what I do not know. Our business quickly grew to the point that we needed some help. So, we hired our first team member. At that moment, I realized the decisions I made as a leader no longer just affected me and my family. They now affected somebody else's family, and I became aware that I did not know much about leading other people. I realized I did not know how to make good business decisions. This awareness started my hunger to grow, so I began reading the books; I went to the courses, the seminars, the webinars, and the conferences. I did everything I knew I could do to grow and learn.

The next phase is where *I know and grow, and it starts to show*. I realized that as I started reading books and attending conferences, seminars, and webinars, I gained knowledge and information. I was learning what it means to be a leader and how to make business decisions. My growth became evident, and others began to take notice. Others would often approach me and ask, "Hey, what are you reading right now?" or "What are you listening to right now?" There was outward evidence that I was growing, and then people would come to me and ask me for advice. There was evidence of growth in my life, which caused others to say, "I see a change in you; there's something different about you; what are you doing?"

I had this head knowledge and started to apply some of the things I was learning. As a side note, in this phase, I was consuming everything I could find. I was reading all the books and listening to all the podcasts, but I started noticing something interesting. Although some of the principles were the same, what some people were saying seemingly contradicted others. What worked for one person did not work for another, so they tried something else, but I was trying to apply all these things simultaneously. It really led to a lot of confusion. I decided I had to determine my vision, I had to determine where I wanted to go, and then I had to determine what my values were and what my core principles would be. That would help me determine the main areas I wanted to grow in and filter who I listened to. Once I determined my vision and values, I started listening to only a few voices for a season. I read their books, I listened to their podcasts, and for me, I dove deeper into the Word. In that season, people would come to me with book suggestions, but I lovingly and kindly responded with, "I appreciate that, but this is not the season for me."

Becoming A Leader Worth Following Through the Process

I was trying to build my foundation so that I could begin to filter other information through. Once I built my foundation, I began to branch out into other sources, but I filtered what I was reading through my foundation. So, if you've got that hunger to grow, develop, and learn everything, I suggest figuring out your vision and values and then finding somebody farther down the path than you in those areas and listening to them for a season.

Step four is *I simply go because I know*. This is when it transitions from the head to the heart. It's no longer just mental activity, but it becomes a part of who you are; it is in you. It goes from head knowledge to a life lived out. It just springs out of you. It flows out of you. In leadership, we teach that leadership is both taught and caught. The taught part is simply the information part. It's the knowledge and the information. Pretty much anybody can read a book and regurgitate information. If you're thinking about Scripture, anybody can memorize a few verses of Scripture and then repeat it back to somebody. But the caught part is the spirit in which the information is taught. It's no longer just the head knowledge, but it is in you. It's a life of experience, and that experience lived out. It's the information that is expressed through you, and that's what people catch. It's the contagious part of you. We can all tell when someone is simply regurgitating information or if that maybe they are in the process of learning and growing. We can also tell when people are sharing an experience that they have lived out. That is powerful when you can connect with somebody who's got the taught and the caught part. That is what this fourth phase is all about. I simply go because of what I know.

I lead a men's Bible study on Tuesday morning, and in one of our recent times together, one of the men said something that I thought was so powerful and profound. He was talking about the Lord's Prayer. He began to speak the Lord's Prayer:

Our Father
who art in heaven
Hallowed Be Your Name
Your Kingdom Come
your will be done

in the Earth as it is in heaven
give us this day our daily bread
and forgive our trespasses
as we forgive those who trespass against us.

But when he finished, he said something that really jumped out to me. He said most translations read, "Your kingdom come, Your will be done *on* the Earth as it is in heaven," but in the original language, it says, "Your kingdom come, your will be done *in* the Earth as it is in heaven." The difference between the words *on* and *in* does not sound so profound on the surface, but there's a huge difference. See, when something gets *in* you, it moves from head knowledge to inside you; it becomes a part of you. It's your operating system. It moves us from just memorizing verses to living those verses out and believing them.

That's when it is *in* you, and that's how it gets *into* the world. In the leadership lane, that's when you're starting to learn leadership principles, apply them, and gain experience, and then you start living it out; it flows from you. That's when it is *in* you.

From the pit to the palace, there's a process, and it's in that process that you and I are refined to become the type of leader that other people willfully follow because of who we are and what we represent. I hope every single one of you will develop into wise men and women who lead at a very high level. This world needs leaders who have pure hearts and pure hands and who lead from a place of pure love. We need those types of leaders to lead at a high level in all streams of society.

What phase of growth would you say you are in right now?

What can you do to go to the next phase of growth?

Day 21

Releasing Breakthrough

"A wise man scales a city of the mighty and brings down the stronghold in which they trust. A warrior filled with wisdom ascends into the high place and releases regional breakthrough bring down the stronghold of the mighty." – Proverbs 21:22 TPT

It's time for us leaders to learn how to wage war and battle. It's the wise warrior who can go up against the might of a city or the enemy's strength—wise, as in being fully led by the Spirit. God gave Joshua and Gideon battle plans that no human intellect could have created. So, it's about surrendering my intellect and desires, submitting to the Word of the Lord, and thoroughly moving forward.

Ephesians 6 says that our battle is not against flesh and blood but against rulers, powers, world forces of darkness, and spiritual forces of wickedness in heavenly places. So, our current battle to bring down the strongholds of our cities, regions, states, and nations is actually on the spiritual plane, not the physical. One of the primary strongholds we face is the mindset that has been twisted and filled with immoral passions.

2 Corinthians 10:3-5: "For though we live in the world, we do not wage war as the world does. The weapons we fight with are not the weapons of the world. On the contrary, they have the divine power to demolish strongholds. We demolish arguments and every pretension that sets itself up against the knowledge of God, and we take captive every thought to make it obedient to Christ." Since the weapons of our warfare are not flesh but

are powerful through God for the demolition of strongholds, we can demolish every deceptive argument that opposes God and break through every arrogant attitude raised up in defiance of the true knowledge of God. We capture, like prisoners of war, every thought and insist it bow in obedience to the Anointed One. We stand ready to punish any trace of rebellion.

We've taken several lines to build the case that the strongholds many of us battle regularly are the mindsets we are entrenched in, whether through our pride, intellect, philosophies, or past programming. I want to get practical here. Paul says to renew our mind in Romans and to renew the spirit of our mind in Ephesians. How do we renew our minds?

We first must understand how the mind works. Our conscious mind can reason inductively and deductively, but the subconscious part of our mind can only reason deductively. The subconscious part of our mind is where our opinions, perceptions, habits, and beliefs lie, and our beliefs drive our behavior. Because your subconscious reasons deductively, it has a conclusion, which is a stronghold or belief, then it finds all the evidence to support it. This can be used for you, or it can be used against you. Most of the time, we allow it to be used against us as negative strongholds.

Here is a personal example; if I say I want to become an internationally recognized author, speaker, and leadership trainer, then this part of my mind says, *How will you do that? Remember, you are a quitter. You quit when things are going well and when things are going poorly. Remember when you had your physical therapy clinics and gyms, and they were extremely impactful, but then you decided to quit? Do you remember that? Do you remember the multi-story mixed used building you were going to build in downtown Tupelo, MS, and how you made a public announcement to let everyone know about it? Do you remember how you were going to name it "The Legacy?" You remember what happened, don't you? You quit when things got challenging and tough. You are a quitter. How are you going to do that?*

This part of me has a stronghold that says I am a quitter; it then finds all the evidence and facts to support this conclusion. So how do I demolish this stronghold? I first ask the Holy Spirit to reveal His truth to me. As I asked the Holy Spirit to reveal His truth in this particular instance, He reminded me that one of the initial goals of opening our physical therapy clinic and our gyms was to make an impact on our community and to see our small-town of 1100 people become one of the healthiest small towns in the state of Mississippi. In 2017, the year we sold our businesses, that town was recognized and awarded a grant by Blue Cross Blue Shield as one of the healthiest small towns in Mississippi. So, we did not quit; the mission had been accomplished. The thing we wanted to establish had been established. When I asked the Holy Spirit to reveal His perspective and truth about the building we had planned to build, He reminded me that when we made our announcement, there were no such buildings in downtown Tupelo, and it was a brand-new concept. In fact, when I met with the city, they said they had been waiting and planning for 20 years for something like this to be built. A few months after our announcement, a developer announced that he also planned to develop a mixed-use building. And since he knew what he was doing, he got started immediately. Within two years, we saw seven similar buildings constructed or in the process of being constructed. So, the truth the Holy Spirit revealed to me is that I made an announcement that was a trigger event that changed the landscape of downtown Tupelo. It caused others to act on the great plans and ideas they had in mind. So, I am not a quitter; in fact, I am a catalyst for transformation.

I now take this evidence and build a case for myself against myself to demolish this stronghold that stands in my way and attempts to hold me back from doing all that God has called me to do. I use this evidence to tear down this stronghold or lie that says I am a quitter.

Our enemy is like a roaring lion looking to steal, kill, and destroy our identity as sons and daughters. He does this in many ways, but one of his primary tactics is through these established strongholds which we have allowed to be built up into a belief system. You have strongholds that have become a lid and cap on the potential impact you can make in the world as a leader. These strongholds are lies and deceptive arguments that oppose

God and directly oppose who He says you are. To demolish these strongholds, we must first become aware of the specific ones in our lives. These strongholds often present themselves as fleeting thoughts, such as *Who do you think you are? How do you think you will do that? Someone else can do that, but that's not for you. You're being arrogant and prideful by stepping out. You'll never measure up. You know it won't be done right or good enough. You're too old or too young. You don't have enough money or time. What will someone think? You're not smart enough to do something like that.* The list goes on, but you get my point.

The first step in pulling down these strongholds is to become aware of the strongholds you have. Once you become aware of them, replace them with the promises and Truth in the Word and what the Holy Spirit reveals to you. We use these Truths as weapons of our warfare. So, when this stronghold makes its presence known, you simply destroy it by responding with Scripture:

> "I am more than a conqueror that has the Presence of God living within me, and He is greater than anything outside of me." (Romans 8:37, Colossians 1:27, 1 John 4:4)

> "I am smart enough; in fact, I have wisdom beyond this world. I have been gifted with the mind of Christ." (1 Corinthians 2:16)

> "I am a magnet for blessing. Surely goodness and mercy follow me all the days of my life." (Psalm 23:6)

> "I am empowered by Christ to bring forward all that He has called me to." (Philippians 4:13, Colossians 1:11, Ephesians 3:16-17)

Those are just a few scriptures you can use to tear down the lies and strongholds in your life and replace them with Truth. There are many other promises all throughout the Word of God; pick some and use them as your weapons.

What are some of the lies you have bought into? What Truths can you use to replace those lies?

Day 22

Default Mode

*"For I'm releasing these words to you this day, yes,
even to you, so that your living hope will be found in
God alone, for He is the only One who is always true."*
– Proverbs 22:19 TPT

In the summer of 2022, we checked a goal off our family bucket list...a 30-day vacation! It was an awesome time and, honestly, one of those goals we wrote down several years ago that we thought would be impossible to ever become a reality. And in the season we wrote the goal, it was an impossibility, but we can discuss turning an idea into reality another time. One night during our vacation, as we were winding down the day and getting ready to go to bed, our youngest son, Brady, started saying that he was not feeling well and that his "tummy hurt bad." So, I suggested that we pray about it, and he agreed. I laid my hand on his stomach and prayed that the pain would go away in the name of Jesus and that he could have a good night of rest. Immediately after we prayed, I asked him how his stomach felt. He initially hesitantly said, "Maybe some better," but then, almost surprised, he said, "Actually, it feels much better." The next morning, he woke up from a great night of sleep. He was playing on his iPad as my wife walked through the living room of our condo into the kitchen. She made the subtle comment that her stomach was not feeling good. Without missing a beat and even looking up from his iPad, Brady suggested, "Just pray about it; you should just pray about it." I kinda chuckled to myself, but I love that! I desire for my personal default mode for anything is to turn to our Father in prayer, and I desire the default mode of our family to be the same.

In 2 Chronicles 14, King Abijah has died, and his son Asa becomes king of Judah. Verse 2 says that Asa did what was good and right in the eyes of the Lord, his God. He led the people back to the Lord, they built cities, and they prospered. There was peace in the land until Zerah the Ethiopian came out against Asa with one million soldiers and 300 chariots, while Asa merely had 580,000 soldiers. They were outnumbered almost 2:1, so Asa turned to God and cried out to Him, saying, "O Lord God, there is none besides you to help, and it makes no difference to You whether the one You help is mighty or powerless. Help us, O Lord our God. Let no man prevail against you!" Asa and his army went on to totally defeat their enemies. In chapter 15 of 2 Chronicles, we see Asa turn once again to the Lord in making national reforms to turn the nation back to the heart of the Lord. He repaired the altar, instituted the daily sacrifice, tore down the Asherah pole, and even removed his own mom from her position of honor as queen mother because she made an image of a false god. Because Asa's default mode was to turn to the Lord, the nation prospered and was at rest...until the 35th year of his reign. Something interesting happened in the 36th year of King Asa's reign. Israel came out against Asa and Judah, and instead of turning to the Lord, Asa went into the treasury in the House of the Lord, took some gold and silver, and sent it to the king of Syria to become allies. Through this alliance, King Asa and Judah were able to defeat Israel, but check out verses 7-10:

> "Because you have put your trust in the king of Aram
> instead of in the Lord your God, you missed your
> chance to destroy the army of the king of Aram. *Don't
> you remember what happened to the Ethiopians and
> Libyans and their vast army, with all their chariots
> and charioteers? At that time, you relied on the Lord,
> and he handed them over to you. *The eyes of the Lord
> search the whole earth to strengthen those whose
> hearts are fully committed to him. What a fool you

have been! From now on, you will be at war. ¹⁰Asa
became so angry with Hanani for saying this that he
threw him into prison and put him in stocks. At that
time, Asa also oppressed some of his people." (NLT)

Wow, what a change in heart posture! While he depended upon God, he was at rest, and the nation prospered, but when his dependency was placed elsewhere, rest was replaced with war, and peace was replaced with oppression. Check out what happened toward the end of Asa's life according to verses 12 and 13:

"¹²In the thirty-ninth year of his reign, Asa developed
a serious foot disease. Yet even with the severity of
his disease, he did not seek the Lord's help but turned
only to his physicians. ¹³So he died in the forty-first
year of his reign." (NLT)

Even in his sickness, Asa did not turn to the Lord but to the physicians first. We have come so far in medicine that there is an easy fix for anything and a pill for everything. "I've got a hurt back; let me get some Tylenol." That has become our default mode, but God is the Great Physician, the Great healer. I'm all for medicine; my background is in the medical profession, and I owned two physical therapy practices. However, our default mode should be to turn to the Lord, no matter how insignificant or how large the matter is. I know we often fear or falsely believe that God is glorified in sickness; we say, "Well, maybe me carrying this sickness is a testimony for God." God is glorified in our breakthrough, not our sickness.

In 2022, I went on a mission trip to Birmingham, AL. One night, we were ministering, and after worship, we began to pray for those who wanted prayer. This other gentleman and I saw a lady sitting on a bench with her hand raised, requesting prayer. As we asked her how we could pray for her, she mentioned that she had had leg pain for several years due to an autoimmune disease, which caused her difficulty standing up without support. She could not close her right hand to make a fist. So, we prayed for her, and after our prayer, we asked her what her pain was like. She said it had gone down from an 8/10 to about a 7/10 but still could not close her hand. We asked if we could pray again, and she said yes. After this second time, she said the pain was the same, and she could tell no difference, but then she said, "Well, I guess I am just someone who needs to carry my pain as a testimony." When she said that, I honestly thought what she said sounded legitimate, but the gentleman with me completely disagreed. He shook his head, looked directly into her eyes, and said with love, "That is not true." She immediately broke down in tears, and as she disagreed with that thought, she was healed. Her pain went down to 0, she could stand without us helping her, and she began closing her hand in a fist without restriction. It was amazing to see God show up. I saw her later that night and asked her how she felt, and with a huge smile spread across, she opened and closed her hand freely without pain and said she felt great. Wow!

The leadership principle I hope you see in this is that God cares for you; He cares who you lead and what you lead. And as you lead, you do not have to rely on your own understanding. He can give you wise plans and solutions to the problems and challenges you face and the opportunities to seize. Even when the challenges or problems appear insurmountable, God can provide a way when there seems to be no way.

Take an honest assessment of how you have responded when challenges popped up. What has your default mode been up until now? Has it been to rely on your own thoughts? Has it been to look at what others in your industry are doing? Has your first response been to go to the Lord?

What current challenge or question are you facing that you could turn to the Lord and seek His guidance on?

Day 23

"God Provides Even While We Sleep"

"Don't wear yourself out trying to get rich. Be wise enough to know when to quit. In the blink of an eye wealth disappears, for it will sprout wings and fly away like an eagle." – Proverbs 23: 4-5 (NLT)

I once heard a guy ask, "How much money is too much money for one individual to have?" As I heard this question, my mind raced back to a complaint I often heard growing up about the excessive money professional athletes earned. The statement would often be along the lines of "No one is worth that much money." In reality, someone saw the value in that individual and was willing to give them a nice amount of money in exchange for their talents. The person writing the check was obviously receiving something of greater value in order to write that check. People do not want to pay for average but gladly and willfully pay for exceptional.

Proverbs touches on this when it says, "Do you see a man skillful in his work? He will stand before kings, he will not stand before obscure men." (Proverbs 22:29) and "A man's gifts make room for him and brings him before the great." (Proverbs 18:21, 14:24) Overall, Proverbs paints a positive picture on wealth and promises: wealth as a reward for wisdom (8:21, 14:24), for righteousness (15:6), generosity (11:25), and diligence (10:4, 12:27). So, is pursuing wealth as a leader a bad thing?

The answer the guy gave to our opening question is the key. How much money is too much money for one individual to earn? Is it $5,000/month? Is it $50,000/month? Is it $500,000/

month?

The answer: whatever amount that replaces trust. Whatever amount that causes us to trust in money over Jesus. Whatever amount that causes us to trust in that amount as our foundation and security over Jesus is too much. For some leaders, that amount is simply having $1,000 in the bank, but for others, they could have an account with $10,000,000 that is compounding, yet their trust is still in the name above all names, Jesus.

This proverb warns against making money and gaining wealth our main focus. Wherever our focus goes, that is where our energy is going to flow. That is why Jesus said we cannot serve two masters. We cannot split our focus. When our focus and energy flow to gaining wealth, we lose our focus on other people and things that deserve our attention.

Gain all the wealth you can but not at the expense of sacrificing your relationship with Jesus, your family, your friends, your health, or all those that look to you for leadership. That is far too high of a price to be paid. It is not worth that sacrifice. Jesus gave us a promise, and He fulfills His promises. He said that we should seek first His kingdom then all these other things will be added. The moment I begin to focus on all these things is the moment I lose focus.

A mentor once told me, "Cory, if you show me your datebook and your checkbook, then I can tell you where you will be one year from now and what you truly value." That was a very powerful statement for me because where you spend your money shows what you think is important, and where you spend your time reveals your habits. The habits and actions we take always produce a result. Where we spend our time reveals what we are willing to trade our time for. Anytime we do anything, we are literally trading our life away for that activity because time is something we will never get back. So, ensure where you spend your time is a worthy trade. Where are you focusing your time and money right now? If I were to look at your datebook and checkbook from the previous 365 days, what would I say you truly value, and what word would I use to describe your habits?

This proverb is really about trust. What are we putting our trust in? Are we trusting in our ability to make something happen or patiently and obediently listening to what the Lord says? Do we continue to work and work and work to ensure we have a healthy bank account and a feeling of security?

So, do not weary and wear yourself out for riches, wealth, fame, security as defined by the world, etc., because Psalms 127:2 says that God can provide for you even while you are asleep.

"It really is senseless to work so hard from early morning till late at night, toiling to make a living for fear of not having enough. God can provide for his lovers even while they sleep!" – Psalms 127:2 (TPT)

That is incredible! God can take care of all that stuff! I have many stories, but I want to briefly share two. These two examples are just an aerial view of what happened. When my wife and I married, we were responsible for many of the costs. We were in college as the wedding day approached and lacked $100 to finish paying for all the costs, and we had no idea how we would be able to pay that last amount. My wife was a full-time student, played college softball, and still had a part-time job. One afternoon just weeks before the deadline for our payment was due, she randomly found a $100 bill lying on the ground!

Another example: as my wife was finishing her doctorate in school, I was working, and we planned to move across the country from Mississippi to Phoenix, AZ, for the last six months of her college. We had everything packed up and ready for the move, and the day before we left, she randomly and completely unexpectedly received a $1,000 scholarship. Needless to say, we were blown away and excited about how we would use this newfound money for our own purposes and fun activities. However, after a series of very unfortunate events, it became very clear that we needed that $1,000 for necessities such as food, gas, and rent.

God is good, and He has great thoughts toward you. He wants to provide for you and your needs. I also believe He wants to provide for your desires because He loves you and deeply cares about you.

The Lord provides for those He loves even while they are asleep.

So, put your trust in Him and do all your work and leading with excellence as if it were for Him, and trust that He will reward you. Trust that He will position you well and that He will open doors that you know nothing about.

Who or what are you putting your trust in?

What do your datebook and checkbook say about you?

Day 24

Made to Run with Horses

"If you faint in your day of adversity, your strength is small." Proverbs 24:10 ESV

What is your response when adversity strikes? Do you throw a hissy fit and complain? Do you get frustrated and give up? Do you diligently seek the Lord? Do you seek the advice and opinions of wise counsel? Do you look for opportunities? Do you start asking *why me*? How do you typically respond?

There are three phrases that leaders never get to use and should immediately be taken out of their vocabulary.

1. "Because I said so." We must give context. When people know why we are doing what we do, they buy in much faster. We also empower them to be better decision-makers.
2. "Do as I say, not as I do." As leaders, our actions and words must align.
3. "Why me?" If there were no challenges, then there would be no need for leadership. This phrase should be changed to *why not me*? You were made for such a time as this. You were made to do hard things.

We all display confidence and a good attitude during times of blessings, but strength and character are put on display through the trials of life. Our ability or inability to stand under pressure shows where our strength truly lies.

In Jeremiah 12, Jeremiah is complaining to God about how the wicked prosper and live a life of ease. He says these people talk about Him with their mouths, but their hearts are far from Him. Then he says, "Look at me, Lord, you know me; you know my heart; you see me," then says, "I mean, how long will you allow this to go on?" Check out the Father's response in Jeremiah 12:5 NLT:

> "If racing against mere men makes you tired,
>   how will you race against horses?
> If you stumble and fall on open ground,
>   what will you do in the thickets near the Jordan?"

God asked Jeremiah, "If you get so tired of these small challenges, how will you ever be able to face the big ones?"

We know that world champion athletes put their bodies through tremendous discipline and stress to compete and win on the world stage. Adversity is your training ground. You can feel that Jeremiah was frustrated and discouraged. Father God responded, "Jerry, I have made you to run with horses, but you are getting tired running with regular runners. I created you to do the hard things, but you are stumbling in a peaceful setting. Get your focus off your circumstances and look to me."

> "Now all discipline seems to be painful at the time,
> yet later it will produce a transformation of character,
> bringing a harvest of righteousness and peace to
> those who yield to it. So be made strong even in your
> weakness by lifting up your tired hands in prayer and
> worship. And strengthen your weak knees." – Hebrews
> 12:11-12.

Just keep building.

> "Do not fret because of evildoers, or be envious of the
> wicked; for there will be no future for the evil man; the
> lamp of the wicked will be put out." -Proverbs. 24:19-
> 20

The word *fret* means "to burn or glow with heat." It's the expression of being angry or overly offended. It's clear that the values of leaders influenced by worldly thinking are different. If you allow your eyes to focus on them instead of what you've been called to build, it's easy to fall into the trap of anger and envy. Such thinking is short-sighted. Whatever the evil build will come to an end. It's only short-sighted; however, as a Kingdom leader, you are building something of greater and lasting value. The Passion Translation of Proverbs 24:3 says that wise people are builders; they build families, businesses, and communities, and through intelligence and insight, their enterprises are established and endure.

Keep building something that will impact generations to come. When we focus our gaze on leaders who build corruptly and seem to be getting ahead, it takes us off a path of legacy and onto a path of distraction which causes us to become "fretful" or angry. If we really get to the root of our anger in this situation, it's anger not only toward the corrupt leader but toward God, who seemingly is allowing pseudo-success to take place. This kind of anger easily leads to envy. Envy is a resentful longing aroused by someone else's possession, qualities, or luck. Finding ourselves on this path changes the ways and values governing how we lead, and we mimic the leadership of the wicked. As you build, you may glance at the short-sighted success path of the wicked but don't linger. Keep your focus forward on building something of lasting value. Keep building.

How do you typically respond to adversity?

What may need to change?

Day 25

God's Secret Counsel

"It is the glory of God to conceal a matter. But the glory of kings is to search out a matter." -Proverbs 25:1

This is a really interesting Proverb to read. But there are other verses throughout the Bible that suggest God has "secrets" that He will gladly reveal to those humble and hungry, those who desire to see Him glorified and not themselves, and those willing to ask, seek, and knock. Just check out some of these:

"The secret of the Lord is with those who fear Him, and He will show them His covenant." -Psalms 25:14

"Call to Me, and I will answer you, and show you great and might things, which you do not know." -Jeremiah 33:3

"He stores up sound wisdom for the upright; He is a shield to those who walk uprightly." -Proverbs 2:7

"For the perverse person is an abomination to the Lord, but His secret counsel is with the upright." -Proverbs 3:32

"The Lord our God has secrets known to no one. We are not accountable for them, but we and our children are accountable forever for all that He has revealed to us, so that we may obey all the terms of these instructions." -Deuteronomy 29:29 NLT

God does not hide things from us, but for us. God is infinite, and His ways and thoughts far exceed our comprehension. Some things are hidden because we are not yet ready to handle the weight that comes with the revelation, but our journey of discovery strengthens our ability to handle it.

For as long as I can remember, there has been this burning desire within me to do something great; it has been deep within me calling me forward, and I do not have the language to put this feeling into words. You are a leader; many of you reading this know exactly what I am talking about. I can remember exactly where I was when this desire began to burn. I was working as a physical therapy assistant at a clinic in Jackson, MS. I had been praying about what in the world this feeling was for several weeks. One day, I was working in the pool room of our clinic with a patient. The pool room was all glass, so I could also see out into the main gym area while in the pool room. I noticed a lady riding an arm bike who appeared happily zoned out. She then looked over at me and, with a surprised look, began waving to me to come to her. As I walked over to her, she told me she was just riding away, deep in prayer and praise, but then looked at me. She said she noticed my shoes, and this thought came to her, "Wow, he sure does have some big feet for such a short white boy." I chuckled. She said, "But as I thought that, the Lord immediately spoke to me and said for me to tell you, 'Yes, he has big feet for where I want him to go, but for right now, he needs to be still.'"

Later that evening, I went home to our apartment. My wife had been placing random sticky notes all over the apartment. When I sat down at the computer, I noticed a sticky note that said Psalm 46:10: "Be still and know that I am God...." God was answering my praying by saying, "Yes, there is a desire that I placed within you, but at this moment, I need you to be still, get to know me more intimately, and let me guide you." If God had revealed that over the next five years, we would open up two physical therapy clinics, four gyms, and have three kids, I would have collapsed under the weight of "How can I?" or "Who am I?" It would have honestly held me back.

It was in the development journey that we became capable

entrepreneurs, but more importantly, in that journey, God revealed more of Himself to us. Up until then, I only knew Him as Lord and Savior. So, when I spoke of Jesus to others, that was the way I presented Him. It was based on my current revelation of His character. But as I sought Him more, he revealed more of Himself and His truths. I began to know Him as a good Father, a counselor, a provider, a healer, an all-powerful revealer of truth. I learned more about His character on this journey, and there's much more to be discovered.

Psalms 103:7 says that God made known His ways to Moses and His acts to the children of Israel. The children of Israel saw what God was doing; they saw His acts, but Moses knew why. God revealed His ways to Moses because Moses pressed in and drew near. He has so much for you that He desires to reveal to you. He has great plans for your family, what and who you lead, and your community. I believe He wants to reveal that to you and is willing to reveal that to you if you press in to Him.

I will end this chapter with one last thought. I was studying Psalms 103:7 one morning, and I was praying that God would make known His ways to me and share His desires for our city, family, and state with me. God broke through my prayers and asked me, "Can you be trusted?"

Can you be trusted to steward well the revelation God gives? As Deuteronomy 29:29 says, we are not accountable for the things that He has not revealed to us, but we are accountable for the things He does reveal. We are accountable to steward well what He does reveal. We must act on it and get it into us and pass it on to the next generation.

Day 26

Blazing Fire

"Where there is no wood, the fire goes out, and where there is no whisperer or gossiper, contentions cease."
– Proverbs 26:20

One of the things required to keep a fire going is a source of fuel. Without a source of fuel, the fire will quickly be quenched. One of the primary sources of strife, anger, contentions, and broken relationships is gossip.

Let's just get real for a moment; gossip is easy to get caught up in. That's why we call it juicy gossip. It's tantalizingly fun to enter into, but a string of broken relationships is left when the fun is over. Gossip is typically based on hearsay and half-truths and ultimately wreaks havoc on relationships. It's idle talk or casual chatter about someone else. In Romans 1, gossip is included in the list of wickedness and sin, along with greed, hate, envy, murder, quarreling, deception, and malicious behavior. Gossipers are like people who just sit around waiting for people to fall or make a mistake so they can quickly tell someone else what they heard or saw.

For the man or woman of honor, gossip should have no place in your heart. So, are you someone who enjoys keeping that strange fire going, or have you determined to be a quencher of that kind of fire? Have you determined to be a leader who lifts people up, not tear them down, a leader who desires to see relationships restored, not torn apart? The way we talk about people is like a peek into the window of our hearts. It's peering behind the curtain of what's on the inside. We want to be men and women of honor who outdo one another in how we honor others with our words.

I love what pastor Bill Johnson says about gossip. He says gossip is a foul misuse of our ability to bring life. Wow, that is so powerful and so true. Our words carry life, have the potential to create, and have the ability to plant seeds of possibility into the imagination of those we lead. Most people do not see the potential within themselves and need a leader to introduce them to that potential. Every great leader I have met or read about has a similar story that revolves around this saying: "[He or she] believed in me before I believed in me." In fact, you probably have some version of that story in your life, where someone came alongside you and believed in you before you believed in yourself. The majority of people start on the borrowed belief of other people. Leaders are belief makers, and we want to be men and women who instill belief.

We want to champion and believe in other people and help others see the greatness within them. But I must make you aware of something; it's easy to champion and believe in someone when they are already amazing and doing incredible things. It's a whole other thing to believe in people before they show the attributes of greatness. It's different believing in people and trusting them before they deserve it. Two Biblical examples immediately come to mind for me. The first example is David before he became King of Israel. He was running for his life, and all the folks who were in debt and running for their lives, those who were distressed, and all those who were discontented came to him. The culture of that day would consider them scoundrels and outcasts. That was their reputation when they came to David. But when they are described later, they are called mighty men of valor and giant killers with phenomenal bravery and exploits. David turned scoundrels into giant killers.

The second example is Jesus. Jesus could have recruited the prestigious, the powerful, or those who were religious and had everything already figured out to be His world changers. Instead, He went to the ordinary and the outcast. He called the fishermen who had to get their hands dirty for a living. He went to the tax collectors, the ones despised by culture. He treated women with honor and respect, which was counter-cultural. He even called the murderers. One of his main guys in the twelve was called a zealot, someone zealous for the nation of Israel; they were trained assassins. They were trained to kill folks, yet Jesus had him as one of his top dudes. Jesus took the outcasts and turned them into world changers. That's amazing, but I must be honest about something. This is a very high reward but also a *very high risk*. The same culture that produced world changers like Peter, James, and John also produced Judas, the betrayer. Championing and believing other people is a high risk, high reward. Because when we champion other people, we must get close to them, which means we also open ourselves up to be used, abused, and accused as leaders. High risk/High reward. Many leaders choose to keep people at a distance and say, "I will not get close to the people I lead." Or maybe they say, "I tried that in the past and got burned. So, I will never do that again." However, when we choose not to get close to those we lead, we may protect ourselves from getting hurt or taken advantage of, but we also decide to never build a great work or to develop great people. To build great people, we must get close to them and believe in people before they show the attributes of greatness.

To close out this chapter, I want to share with you a term that is new to me. It's called "glory gossip." Glory gossiping is bragging about others and verbally honoring others. We don't want to be known for talking about people behind their backs, but we do want to be known for bragging about people behind their backs. As leaders, we must steward well the people we lead, but we also must steward well the words that flow from our lips.

Up until now, how intentional with your words have you been? What do you feel needs to change in your use of your words?

Day 27

Take up the Responsibility

"Like a bird that wanders from her nest, so is a man who wanders from his home." – Proverbs 27:8

The bird that wanders from the nest she made for her family may fear certain threats or search for something more exciting. The man that wanders from his home may wander for the same reasons: fear or the pursuit of a perceived excitement, yet they both result in the abandonment of responsibility.

The word for *home* has a few possible meanings, but all are applicable: a place to live, a city, a specific location, or a region. It could also refer to a standing place, office, or post as in a role or title. The man or woman who wanders has taken their eye off the true goal and has laid down their God-given responsibility, choosing to either flee in fear or pursue another shiny object. They have SOS (shiny object syndrome).

To wander due to fear is inexcusable. Fear is faith in the wrong God. Do we often get the emotion of fear? Yes, of course! But if we give into that fear, we demonstrate that our confidence is placed in someone or something outside of God. Proverbs 28:1 says the wicked flee; they run away even when no one is chasing them. They run in fear of something they created in their imagination. Yet the righteous are as bold as lions. The righteous stand on a firm foundation, their hearts being settled into the loving hands of the Father so they can stand boldly.

I find it interesting that in this particular proverb, the word for man is not the word "adam," which generally refers to mankind, but a word that refers to a husband or someone who is supposed to be in covenant. For the wanderer, although a covenant has been established, the commitment to it has not sunk in at the heart level. I believe God has a people, a place, and a purpose for each of our lives. That's what Acts 17:26 refers to. It says that God created each person, and beforehand He decided when they would live and the boundaries in which they would live. That means you could have been created at any point in history. You could have been created 1000 years ago or 1000 years from now, yet here you are. You were made for such a time as this. You were made for such a generation as this, and I believe you were made to be a leader of leaders for such a moment as this. The fact that He determined the boundaries in which you live means that you are in the exact location that He desires you to be. To deny those truths is to lay down your responsibility for your city and your generation.

My wife and I grew up in a town in north Mississippi, but when we got married, we moved away for her college. When she was nearing graduation and pregnant with our first child, we began to seek the Lord for where we should locate our family. We were looking at large metropolitan cities with plenty of activities for active families, such as Austin, Phoenix, and Nashville. But while we were seeking Him, I heard Him clearly say, "Tupelo, MS." I said, "NOOOOOOO, anywhere but Tupelo! Nobody cares about health and fitness, nobody cares about growth and development" (those are both false by the way). He said, "There will be no change unless someone makes a change, so why not you?" We were absolutely amazed and said yes to His call to move back home, and within five years, we had built two physical therapy clinics and four gyms and had three children. God had absolutely blessed us, but something deep within me called for something greater. I remember walking around our neighborhood in prayer. I asked the Lord one question: "Why are we here? We have been here for eleven years now, but why?" He said in such a beautiful way, "Why is the wrong question. The question should not be, why are we here, but what can we do here? And you cannot make a difference if you have indifference in your heart."

WOW! I was blown away. He completely revealed to me how my

heart was still longing to move away and do something somewhere else, anywhere else, when the responsibility He had called us to in that season was to the city where we lived. He showed me that "What can we do here?" is a creative and innovative question that takes on responsibility, while "why" is defensive and passive. And there was indifference deep within my heart that needed to be dealt with. I simply could not impact the lives of others and advance His Kingdom if I did not capture His heart for the city and the people in the city.

I hope this is an encouragement to you. You are not a mistake, and God has a specific purpose and plan for your life. He cares greatly and deeply for you, and He desires for you to experience His love and then be a river, not a reservoir, of His love in your city and the people in your circle of influence.

What are some of the challenges in your city?

Ask the Holy Spirit for some solutions to those challenges?

Take action on what He gives you.

Day 28

Empowered to Advance

"Because of the transgressions of the land, many are its princes. But by a man of understanding and knowledge, right will be prolonged." – Proverbs 28:2 NKJV

If you just read through the books of 1 and 2 Kings, you will find this long list of kings who did evil in the sight of the Lord. In fact, you will see two centuries worth of nine dynasties with twenty different kings. Talk about turnover. I find it very sobering how Jeremiah 10:21 describes those in leadership over his nation:

"For the shepherds have become dull-hearted and have not sought The Lord; therefore, they shall not prosper, and all their flocks shall be scattered."

Many people want to lead, but they do not have the heart to lead. Many want the perks associated with having a title or position, but they do not want to pay the price to be a real leader. They desire the perks of leadership, such as authority, power, recognition, etc., but they do not understand the price because the real price of leadership is to serve people.

When leaders focus on themselves and not those they lead, nations, communities, businesses, and families are thrown into chaos and disorder. Our greatest example of leadership is Jesus, who came to serve. He laid down His life to give life to others. He also demonstrated real leadership in how He trained, equipped, and empowered others. He saw potential and called it out when circumstances said otherwise. He stood up to adversity, challenged the unjust, spoke for truth, and did not cower away. Jesus was fully God and fully man. He was a man of understanding and knowledge. He came to set the captives free, destroy the works of the enemy, restore what was lost by Adam in Genesis, and display the Father. Jesus was the ultimate leader.

Jesus declares a promise in John 16:7 that I absolutely love. He said, "But very truly I tell you, it is for your good that I am going away. Unless I go away, the Advocate will not come to you; but if I go, I will send him to you."

The promise Jesus made was that he would be sending The Holy Spirit. I love the chapters of John 15-17 because these chapters are packed with the promises of God for us. I was praying one morning, and the Lord said, "My promises are the key to a transformed heart and transformed mind." He then asked me, "What do you think would happen if just a small percentage of the church fully believed my promises?" My first thought was, *wow, I wonder what would happen if I fully believed His promises.* I heard a pastor say one time (I cannot remember who said it), but the pastor mentioned that in English, we tend to search the scriptures for specific promises. In Hebrew, the definition of a promise of God is *every time He speaks*. In verse 7 of John 16, Jesus promises to empower His disciples with His Spirit.

I'm going to jump over into the lane of leadership for just a moment. When we teach about the importance of leaders empowering others, we discuss that one is too small of a number to achieve anything great. If you can do whatever you want to do on your own, then you are not dreaming big enough. So, we talk about the importance of empowering others; empowering someone else refers to us giving power away. When we empower others, we see a multiplication factor that kicks in. There is a 5-step empowerment process we talk about in leadership:

1. Step one is *I do it*. To give power away, I must first have power. So, I do the activity. We see throughout the Gospels where Jesus healed the sick, cast out demons, destroyed the works of the enemy, and preached the Kingdom of God. He did it. He demonstrated who He was.
2. Step two is *I do it, and you are with me*. This is where you

are a witness to what I am doing. I do it, and you are with me, but it's not a passive sitting back and watching. I'm teaching you what I am doing and why I am doing it to help you understand. I want to teach you so you can know how to think and not just what to think. I want to teach you how to think so when I hand you the ball, you will know how to think and make decisions. In John 6, Jesus is about the feed the 5000, and he asks Phillip, "Where will we buy bread for these people to eat?" In the next verse, it says that Jesus asked this question to test him because He already knew what He would do. Why would Jesus ask a question that He already knew the answer to? Jesus knew that Phillip and the disciples would carry on His Gospel message once He ascended to heaven. He knew that they would be the ones empowered to advance His kingdom and would come across challenges as well as opportunities. They could think and make decisions from a human perspective, but He taught them they could think from a higher plane. They could offer Kingdom solutions to worldly opportunities and challenges.

3. Step three is *you do it, and I am with you*. This is where I, as the leader, hand the ball off to you for you to practice leadership. I give you the opportunity to put into practice what you have witnessed. Jesus did this when He called the twelve together, then again when He called the seventy together to send them out. He gives them power and authority over all demons to heal diseases and preach the Kingdom of God. When the seventy disciples returned, they were excited to share with Jesus that even the demons submitted to them in His name. Jesus replied, "I saw Satan fall like lightning from heaven" (Luke 10:17-18).

4. Step four is *you do it*. This is where you are empowered. I fully hand the ball off to you for you to run with it. You are now empowered to take ownership. Just before Jesus ascended into heaven, He said to His disciples, "All authority on Heaven and earth has been given to me. Therefore go" (Matthew 28:18). Jesus was saying that He had all authority,

and He empowered them to go in this power and authority to go out as His representatives, as His ambassadors. Go.

5. Most good leaders will stop right there, but truly great leaders know that there is one more step, and that step is where *you do it, and someone else is with you.* There is this continual empowering and equipping down process. The rest of Matthew 28:19 says, "Therefore go and make disciples of all nations, baptizing them in the name of the Father, and of the Son, and of the Holy Spirit." In 2 Timothy 2:2, Paul tells Timothy to take what you have learned from me and teach it to faithful men who can also teach others—Paul to Timothy to faithful leaders to others.

In John 16:7, Jesus tells His disciples that it's to their advantage that He leaves because by Him leaving, they would be empowered by His Spirit to advance His kingdom. Amazingly, He spoke those words to just a handful of individuals in a small spot on the planet, and it has advanced to us here today.

We have been empowered by the Spirit of the Living God to continue to advance His Kingdom, heal the sick, cast out demons, destroy the works of the enemy, display the love of The Father, and preach the good news of the gospel.

What are you doing to intentionally develop yourself?

What are you doing to intentionally develop those you lead?

Day 29

Where Are You Going?

"Where there is no vision, the people perish. But he that keeps the law, happy is he." – Proverbs 29:18 (NKJV)

"When there is no clear prophetic vision, people quickly wander astray. But when you follow the revelation of the Word, Heaven's bliss fills your soul." -Proverbs 29:18 (TPT)

"If people can't see what God is doing, they stumble all over themselves, but when they attend to what He reveals, they are most blessed." -Proverbs 29:18 (MSG)[8]

In Lewis Carroll's famous book, "Alice in Wonderland," the main character, Alice, meets the Cheshire cat. Upon meeting the cat, Alice asks, "Would you tell me, please, which way I ought to go from here." The cat responds, "That depends a good deal on where you want to get to." Alice says back, "I don't much care where." The Cheshire cat then drops some wisdom for Alice and for us, "Then it doesn't much matter which way you go." When asked if there was anything worse than being born blind. Hellen Keller thought about it for a moment and said, "Yes. Being born with sight but no vision."

---

8   Scripture quotations marked MSG are taken from THE MESSAGE, copyright © 1993, 2002, 2018 by Eugene H. Peterson. Used by permission of NavPress. All rights reserved. Represented by Tyndale House Publishers, Inc.

As a leader, there are many things we can delegate, equip, train, and empower others to do, but vision is not one of them. A leader is 100% responsible for three things: casting vision, defining reality, and getting alignment. As it relates to vision, according to Proverbs 29, any city, country, state, family, church, individual, or business that does not have vision will wander aimlessly and go astray. The word *vision* is more than a mission or goal or a simple direction; it's Divine direction. It's prophetic vision given by the Holy Spirit. I must ask myself, *"Am I asking, knocking, and seeking His vision for myself and for what I lead?"* When I don't know what He is saying, I wander aimlessly, and the purpose for which I was created perishes. When I have vision, it gives me direction and helps me to make better decisions. Having a clear vision also allows others to easily say, "Yes, I want to be a part of that," or "No, I don't want to be a part of that." Vision is not the great unifier; it is really the great separator. It separates those on my team who want to accomplish the vision from those who prefer not to go on that journey with us.

There came a time in our physical therapy business when we were growing to the point we needed to hire another therapist to join our team. We had a young lady come in for an interview. In the interview, I shared our vision with her. I told her about the impact we were making within our community and how we were literally witnessing the healthcare of our community change for the better. I told her how we were working with local high school athletes and seeing those athletes win state championships. After I shared this powerful vision with her, she told me that it was not something she was looking for. I was honestly quite shocked.

As I got home and told my wife about this, I asked her a rhetorical question: "How in the world can you claim to be a physical therapist and not want to be a part of what we are doing?" My wife did not see it as rhetorical and responded, "Cory, you have to understand that not everyone wants to be a part of your vision." Wow, that is so wise and so profound. She is right; not everyone will want to be a part of your vision, nor *should* they be a part of your vision. This young lady would have probably performed well and done a good job because she's a professional, but she would never be fully satisfied, and she would not go all in. We are looking for those who want to go all in with us to do amazing things. Having a clear vision allows people to make that decision.

I mentioned that we, as leaders are responsible for three things:

1. Vision. This is the direction we are going. As Kingdom leaders, we can expect and should lean into God's direction.
2. Defining reality. We must define reality as it truly is. Not as we wish it would be, how it could be, or how we think it should have been, but as it is. If vision is where we are going, reality is where we are. To get to where we are going, we must look honestly at our current situation.
3. Get alignment. Alignment is when we ask for commitment. It's when we ask those we lead to co-labor with us by taking some action. We can cast vision, but when we ask for commitment, that's where the rubber meets the road. Many people will say, "Yes, I will," because it may sound good, but sounding good and doing good are not the same thing. Asking for a commitment is how we close the gap between sounding good and doing good. One caveat here is that sometimes the timing is not right. People may like the vision and be bought into it, but it may not be the right season for them to fully participate, and that's ok. When we ask those we lead to commit to taking action, we tend to lose the uncommitted and gain the committed.

I know there have been several chapters throughout this book in which I have shared something about vision, but I hope by now that you see the importance of having a clear vision. If this is an area you are having a hard time with, I help leaders with this as part of my coaching, and I would love the opportunity to work alongside you. Another option for you to consider is to ask yourself a few questions:

What makes me come alive?

What do I truly enjoy doing with my time?

What activity after completing it rejuvenates me?

Where would I love to be six months from now?

Day 30

When the Blessing Becomes a Curse (Idleness)

"God, I'm so weary and worn out, I feel more like a beast than a man. I was made in your image, but I lack understanding." – Proverbs 30:2 TPT

As leaders who bear the weight of great responsibilities and carry the burdens of others, you can probably relate to this Proverb. In the pursuit of excellence and success, weariness can seep into your bones, leaving you feeling more like a beast than the visionary leader you are meant to be.

In your demanding role, it's essential to remember that you were made in the image of God. Your weariness does not diminish your value or negate your purpose. In fact, God longs to reveal His strength and wisdom through you during these moments of weariness.

1 Samuel 30 tells of an extremely stressful moment in the life of David. It was so bad that his own guys considered stoning him to death! But David's response to this stressful situation was interesting. It says that he strengthened himself in the Lord. David chose to draw near to the Lord at that moment.

When weariness threatens to consume you, invite God into your journey. Seek His presence, not just to find solace, but to tap into the limitless reservoir of His strength. Align your perspective with His understanding, for He sees beyond the limitations of the present moment.

As a high-level leader, you have the opportunity to cultivate an environment of renewal and inspiration. But it must start within you. Surrender your weariness and the need for complete understanding to the One who holds all wisdom. Trust that He will equip you with the discernment, insights, and energy you need to navigate the challenges that lie ahead.

Remember, the weariness you experience is not in vain. It is in these moments that your character is shaped and refined. By being humble and depending on God, you will develop a strength surpassing your abilities. This strength will radiate from you, inspiring and uplifting those who look to you for guidance.

A popular leadership/personal growth quote says, "If you don't take control over your calendar, someone else will." This means that your time, if not intentionally taken over, will always be filled sometimes with things you'd rather not be doing. But what would it look like if we allowed a specific Someone to take over our calendar? I mean, He is a good Father; He does have a good plan for your life, so what if we asked Him to fill our day?

I encourage you to implement some kind of reflection process regularly. I have a daily, weekly, quarterly, and yearly reflection process. When we reflect, we allow the lesson of our day to catch up with us, but we also can see where we spend our time. My daily and weekly reflection process looks like this: at the end of each day, I reflect on it and ask myself seven questions. This process takes less than ten minutes, but it helps me hold myself accountable to what I deem important and see where I need to spend more or less time. The seven questions I ask myself are:

1. What did God teach me today?
2. What did I learn today?
3. Did I lead my family well today?
4. Was I wise financially?
5. Did I have a new idea?
6. Did I compromise?
7. What was one win for the day?

At the end of the week, I will look back over my previous week to see the 3-5 biggest wins of the week, then I will look at my upcoming schedule for the week to see where I need to be at my best.

Do you have a reflection process?

Is there an area of your life where you could do a better job of time management?

Day 31

The High Calling of a Leader

"For you are a king, Lemuel, and it's never fitting for a king to be drunk on wine or for rulers to crave alcohol. For when they drink, they forget justice and ignore the rights of those in need, those who depend on you for leadership." – Proverbs 31:4-5 TPT

At the time of this writing, our oldest son has just turned eleven years old, and I recently took him on our "man trip." Since this was his trip, he chose our destination, and because he loves soccer, he chose to go to Atlanta, Georgia, to watch his first MLS soccer match. We had a great time, and the point of this man trip was for us to spend some alone time together and enjoy each other's presence. We had a great time, but I also wanted to be intentional and use this trip to lay out some of our family values. We discussed many of the hot topics I knew he would be facing as he grew from being a little boy to a young man. I wanted him to know that I am for him and desire to see him prosper in God's calling on his life. I also wanted him to know that Google and Siri and any other search engine he may use to find answers to problems, issues, or opportunities he may face along life's journey did not have his best interest in mind, but I wholeheartedly did. So, I wanted him to know he could confidently and comfortably come to me with anything. I also laid out where my wife and I stand on many topics he would encounter, such as premarital sex, drugs, alcohol, and being a Kingdom-minded leader. I walked him through the Bible on why we had those beliefs. Then I told him what culture would say and that he would have to make a choice upfront on where his commitments would lie and what his non-negotiables would be. You must state your non-negotiables before a decision is required and strong emotions are involved. I ultimately want our children to be wise decision-makers. I let him know that the world could live life in direct opposition to what we believe, but that would not change the fact that we value all people and still would not act according to worldly culture. The world could do those things, but we choose not to participate.

At the beginning of Proverbs 31, King Lemuel's mom gives him similar advice. She told him that, no doubt, specific temptations would come his way. He needed to decide upfront that he would not participate in what others may get away with because he now had a position of great influence and responsibility. She encouraged him to use this position to lay himself down in order to serve those he's called to lead. His mom told him that wine is not for a king, that others can participate if they want, and he may have in the past, but it should no longer be his way of life. She said he is now in a role where others depend upon him, and his decisions impact others.

But that begs the question of *why*? Why should others get to have all the 'fun'? Why should others get to do whatever they want to do whenever they want to do it? It's because true leadership is laying aside your self-serving agenda to serve others and lead them into destinies they cannot even fathom. That's the role of a leader.

Leadership is 100% fun, has tons of perks, and often comes with honors and accolades, but it comes at a price. Earlier in the book, we discussed how leaders give up something of a lesser value to gain something of a greater value. This is not a proverb against drinking alcohol; it's a proverb against anything that disrupts the communication line between leaders and the Holy Spirit. Hosea 4:11 in the AMPC says, "Harlotry and wine and new wine that take away the heart and the mind and the spiritual understanding."

Christian leaders should be the wisest, most innovative, and most transformational people on the planet because we have the Spirit of God dwelling within us, and we have the mind of Christ.

The High Calling of a Leader

We can create, innovate, and make decisions based on wisdom not found in the world and not on our intellect but on the wisdom from The Creator Himself. However, we can quench the flow of the Spirit of Wisdom through substances that alter our thinking, shiny objects that take away our focus, and relying upon our own understanding of things.

The importance of having a sound mind as a leader is clear because, as a leader, you will often be making difficult decisions. President Theodore Roosevelt said, "In any moment of decision, the best thing you can do is the right thing, the next best thing you can do is the wrong thing, and the worst thing you can do is nothing." I like that because it's only when we make a choice that we get feedback. Many people have difficulty making decisions because they waver in trying to make the perfect choice, and they fear failure. Often this leads those individuals to do nothing at all. I have found that I never know if the choice is correct until after the decision is made and I have taken the action. Once I take action, feedback is given, and I see that yes, that was the right choice or no, that was not the right choice. If it was the wrong choice, I simply make corrections, but I do not get any of that if I decide not to act.

Author Napoleon Hill says that successful people actually have a habit around how they make decisions. Unsuccessful people do as well. He says that successful people make their decisions quickly and change their minds slowly, while unsuccessful people make their decisions slowly and change their minds quickly. When Napoleon Hill says successful people make their decisions quickly, he does not mean impulsively. Successful people can quickly make decisions by remembering their vision or where they are going, looking at where they currently are by defining the current reality, remembering their values or non-negotiables, and asking wise counsel for perspective. With these four thoughts in mind, they can quickly decide and then only change their mind once it becomes evident they made the wrong choice. They then simply correct the decision. Unsuccessful people make their decisions slowly. I don't think it has anything to do with time but everything to do with procrastination. Unsuccessful people put off making a decision, and when they finally are forced to, they waver.

As we wrap up this chapter, I want to encourage you that as a leader, you set a standard of excellence that others are watching and ultimately may end up following. John Maxwell says, "The only right a leader has to say follow me is if they are worth following." A leader without standards or unwillingness to make decisions is not worth following. Others can live below this standard, but not me or you.

Acts 17:26 says, "and He has made from one blood every nation of men to dwell on all the face of the earth, and *has determined their preappointed times and the boundaries of their dwellings."* That means you could have been created at any point in the timeline of history, yet here you are, leading in the present day. *You were made for such a time as this.* You were made to lead at this moment. You were made to lead at this point in history. You were made to lead in this generation. Acts 13:36 says that when David had served the purpose of God in his own generation, he fell asleep. As David served his generation, you, my friend, are called to lead and serve this generation. That's an incredible truth and an incredible reality.

I know this world needs leaders who lead at a very high level of leadership and influence in every stream of society. Leaders who lead with clean hands and a pure heart. Leaders who stand for truth and justice. Leaders unwilling to be bought, unwilling to be frauds, unwilling to take backroom deals, but leaders who lead from integrity.

What do you feel God is doing in your life and leadership right now?

What do you feel you need to let go of in this season?

Up until now, what have been your habits around decision-making?